TRIPLE YOUR READING SPEED

TRIPLE YOUR READING SPEED

Dr. Wade E. Cutler

President and Director,
Accelerated Education Schools

A Genesis Press Book

arco
New York

Published by ARCO PUBLISHING COMPANY, Inc.
219 Park Avenue South, New York, N. Y. 10003
Copyright © Wade E. Cutler, 1970
Fourth Printing, 1977
All Rights Reserved

Library of Congress Catalog Card Number 70-93503

Printed in the United States of America

Contents

6

Wait!
Before You Start to Read . . .

To get the greatest benefit from this book, *do not* start on the first page of the text (Part I). Get acquainted with the book first.

1. Thoroughly read the outside. (Check the title, the author's name, read the comments on the covers.)
2. Note any information given about the author.
3. Check the publisher's name and the copyright date on back of the main title page.
4. Carefully read the Foreword.
5. Read the Contents page.
6. Thumb through the entire book. (Note the layout.)
7. Note the information contained in the appendices.

Now you are ready to turn to Part I. You know a lot about this book—the subject, the author, the treatment of the topic, the typography, etc. This book has its own individual personality, just the same as each person you know has an individual personality. Get to know the individuality of every book you read. You'll get more from your study. We'll have much more to tell you about previewing in Part II.

Now go on to Part I, page 11.

Foreword

Since 1965, the Cutler Accele*read* Method has been taught successfully to nearly 10,000 persons, both students and adults, primarily in the Southwest.

In-resident classes taught for relatively small study groups have developed dramatic improvements in individual reading rates and comprehension scores. Accelerated Education Schools, the name under which the Accele-*read* Course is marketed exclusively are presently in operation in Texas, New Mexico, and Oklahoma. Schools will open in additional states soon.

The Schools guarantee that a graduate of the program will read 1,000 words per minute, or 3 times the pre-course tested rate (whichever is greater) and with improved comprehension. Research proves that the average rate increase for graduates of the closely supervised, individualized course is from 7 to 12 times, depending upon the individual student's basic ability, the type of material being read, the purpose for which it is read, and other factors.

Comprehension, as measured by objective tests, normally increases an average of 13 percent. However, overall understanding of materials read is usually markedly improved—far more than that measured solely by objective tests.

An integral and important part of the outstanding success of this reading method is the intensive, specialized training and practice in developing better study habits and improved test-taking skills.

This one book contains all the necessary theory, explanation, and study and practice exercises to enable the interested reader to at least triple his present reading rate and improve comprehension if he pursues the program as clearly outlined.

This is a tested and proved method. It is not experimental; it works. You can put the methods described here to valuable use by applying them to accelerate your success and education. Remember: reading is the basis of all education.

You, too, can become an Accelerated Reader!

Part I: Learn About Reading and Yourself

You Can Read Much Faster

If you can read these words, you can read faster. You probably have some doubts. You say that it just isn't possible; that you can only read so fast and that is it. Not true. It is now possible for every reader who applies himself to the guides and materials in this book to triple his present rate and to improve comprehension of what he reads.

What does this mean to you?

It means that you can read *three* books in the time you now require to read one. And you'll understand what you read better.

You'll reduce normal reading fatigue by as much as two-thirds.

You'll better be able to keep up with the required reading of your profession—that paper backlog that gets bigger every week.

You'll be able to read your daily newspaper and magazines in much less time.

You'll have time to read a few of the current best-sellers so that you can discuss them intelligently with friends. It does get embarrassing to always answer in the negative when someone asks if you have read such and such book.

You might even be able to have more leisure time when you become an Accelerated Reader.

These are just a few advantages of reading faster. You'll no doubt add to this list.

Interested?

Read on.

A strong *desire* to improve your reading speed and comprehension is necessary before a marked change is to be noted. If you honestly desire improvement, you will read and practice with the regularity and determination which will help you achieve your goal sooner.

Perhaps you question your ability to succeed in tripling your reading rate. Think about this statement. Psychologists have estimated that the average individual—that's you and me—uses only about 10 percent of his abilities. Ten percent! What a pity to waste some 90 percent! If you are reading at 100 to 300 words per minute now, using 10 percent of your reading ability, how fast could you read if you used 20, 30, 40 or more percent?

That's the purpose of this book—to help you search out, utilize, and perfect the wonderful skills for reading which you already possess, but seldom use effectively. You'll learn how to make your reading and study time more valuable and productive.

In the end, you'll have two choices. You'll be able to markedly reduce the time you now require to do necessary reading, or you'll be able to get much more done in the same amount of time you now require for reading. Either way, YOU are the winner!

Measure Your Rate & Comprehension

Before you begin actual practice in becoming an Accelerated Reader, it is necessary that we take an inventory to determine your present reading rate and comprehensive ability.

The purpose for the two selections which follow is to get as accurate a measure of both reading rate and comprehension as possible. Therefore, you are urged to read each at your normal rate. Keep in mind the fact that following each reading is a thorough test to measure comprehension, so read for good understanding.

In order to time yourself, you will need a watch or clock with a second hand. Be careful to place the timepiece so that you do not try to read it from an angle which could result in an inaccurate computation of your score.

It is best, if possible, to adjust the clock so that the minute and second hands are synchronized. If you have a stopwatch available, all the better.

Select a starting time in advance and note it on the lines below.

Starting Time: MINUTES ———— SECONDS ————

As the second hand reaches the time you have written down, begin reading.

INVENTORY SELECTION 1

Radio Communications and the Sun

by Wade E. Cutler

Through the years man has become more and more critical about carefree and undistorted radio communications, but frequently he finds reception poor or completely impossible. What is the reason?

Radio interference, often the major reason for poor communications, can be widely classified into two groups: (1) That caused by man; and (2) That caused by nature. The disturbances caused by man and man-made machines are numerous; but, overall, are not as important in radio communications as are those disturbances caused by nature. It is not the purpose of this paper to discuss the numerous man-made disturbances with which most radio users are already quite familiar, but to discuss the greatest hamperer of radio communications—the sun—and how it affects radio.

The sun is looked to for many things; in fact, all life is dependent on the sun for its existence. Few radio users are aware of the dominant influence of the sun on radio transmission and reception. For better understanding, an explanation of what happens to a radio wave seems appropriate.

All signaling by means of radio occurs as the result of waves that travel from a transmitter to a receiver. These waves, which are electromagnetic in character, arise from the presence of rapidly alternating currents in the antenna of the transmitter. From the antenna, these waves spread out in all directions with the velocity of light, 186,000 miles per second. The distant receiving antenna intercepts only a small amount of the wave energy that is radiated by the transmitter's antenna. In most instances, this small amount of energy is adequate for satisfactory communication.

The carrier waves which are sent out by the radio station's antenna may be divided into two categories: First, the ground wave; and second, the sky wave. The distance of ground wave travel is limited and, therefore, is seldom of importance for communication over distances of more than a few hundred miles. The sky wave is relied upon for long range communications.

When the receiver is far from the transmitter, say, well around the curve of the earth, transmission and reception would be impossible were it not for the presence of several layers of electricity high above the surface of the earth at altitudes of from 60 to 250 miles. These layers act as "mirrors," reflecting back to earth waves that otherwise would be lost in interplanetary space. This upper region of the atmosphere consists of electrically charged particles originally emitted by the sun, and molecules and atoms whose electrons have been torn from them as the result of ultraviolet radiation. The charged particles are commonly referred to as ions; hence, the reflecting layers are usually referred to as the ionosphere.

Judging from the above, it is evident that the sun is instrumental in forming the layer known as the ionosphere. Although the ionosphere has been referred to as a sort of mirror, it might more accurately be compared to a sieve. This ionosphere sieve which encloses the entire spherical earth is not at all uniform. Over that portion of the earth where the sun's rays strike nearly vertically, the sieve openings are small. This characteristic arises from the fact that in the vertical striking area solar radiation produces the greatest electrification.

The conclusion that radio waves are literally bounced off this "mirror" is a very accurate one. Then it is easy to see that a radio wave, which, instead of bouncing off this electrical field goes through it, would be lost and could not be picked up by the antenna of the receiver. Most of the time the "mesh" of this sieve remains fairly constant, and radio experts have been able to set frequencies of the correct size and length so that they normally bounce as they are intended to do. But frequently they do not bounce, but go right through enlarged sieve openings and are lost in interplanetary space and cannot be detected by the antenna of the receiver. But why do these openings vary in size? Why must they vary even from minute to minute? For the answer, the radio user must look to the sun and its habits.

As has been stated earlier, the sun creates this electrical ionosphere. This layer is formed when ultraviolet light shines upon molecules of oxygen and nitrogen, partly decomposing them, and knocks off little electrons from the atoms creating the so-called ions.

Radio engineers and scientists have ascertained this layer's presence, and can measure its altitude by sending up radio pulses through the stratosphere until they hit the radio ceiling, bounce back, and are caught in the receiving apparatus. The time that it takes the radio wave to go to the ionosphere and back is carefully noted by computing the rate of travel at the velocity of light.

On the side of the earth turned toward the sun, where the ionosphere is constantly exposed to the sun's rays, the ceiling is much lower than on the side of the earth away from the sun. This accounts for the great difference in the way in which radio waves travel in day-time as compared with night-time. The shorter waves, or higher frequencies, are better for day-time transmission, while the longer or lower frequencies are better for night transmission.

Just as there is a day and night effect on transmission, there also is a seasonal effect. During the long summer months, in the northern hemisphere, the top of the atmosphere is much more heavily ionized than during the shorter days in the winter season. The radio ceiling, therefore, is lower in the summer than in the winter. The regular radio user is probably aware that long distance radio reception is usually better in the winter than in the summer. This is due mainly to a higher, more reflective radio ceiling, or ionosphere.

If the sun remained constant, it would be fairly simple to work out charts and plans and in most cases overcome the common failures of radio transmission and reception. But the sun, like all things, is constantly changing. The most noticeable change is the appearance of sunspots.

Sunspots are "dark spots" visible on the sun's surface, and are believed to be tornado-like solar storms. Their average duration is two weeks, and they occur usually in eleven year cycles. Sunspots are in reality storm areas in the solar atmosphere. Like similar cyclonic low pressure disturbances on the earth's surface, they are cooler than their surroundings. The sun's shining surface appears to have a temperature of about 6,000 degrees centigrade; that of sunspots is about 2,000 degrees lower, which is why they appear relatively darker by contrast.

Then how do sunspots affect radio? When, during sunspot maxima, solar activity results, as it generally does, in a greater output of ultraviolet light, the ionosphere is more heavily ionized than during the years of sunspot minima. This results in long undulations of the radio ceiling as it rises and falls over an eleven year period. When a sunspot is suddenly formed, or a violent eruption takes place in the atmosphere of the sun, there is a burst of energy sent toward the earth, which, hitting the ionosphere, may create all sorts of disturbances.

Thus, it is easily seen, in view of the fact that long range reception depends upon the radio sky wave being reflected from the ionosphere, that the sun and radio communications are intimately linked.

Stop. Note exact time and write it in below.

Finishing Time: MINUTES ———— SECONDS ————

HOW TO FIGURE RATE

To determine your reading rate of words per minute, do this: (1) subtract your starting time from your finishing time; (2) convert whole minutes into seconds by multiplying the number of minutes by 60; (3) now add to that total any extra seconds; (4) divide your total seconds into 1,230 (the number of words in the selection). Carry only to the largest single decimal place. Your answer will be something like 2.7 or 3.4, etc. This is your word per *second* rate; (5) now multiply your word per second rate by 60 to determine your word per minute rate. Record the result below.

Selection 1: Reading Rate: ———— w.p.m.

Now answer the following 25 questions covering the selection by circling the letter before the answer which seems most nearly correct. Read each question and each possible answer *carefully*. Careful reading of this test and all tests can result in better scores.

If a question stumps you, skip it and return to it later. Do not leave any question unanswered since you are graded on the number right. An unattempted answer will count as much off as an incorrect response.

The entire test is to be answered totally from recall. Do not look back for an answer.

INVENTORY COMPREHENSION TEST 1

1. In radio communication, man-made disturbances are
   a. important.
   b. unimportant.
   c. numerous.
   d. not as important as are nature's.
   e. both c & d.

2. In order to be effective, all radio waves must travel
   a. from a receiver to a transmitter.
   b. from antenna to antenna.
   c. through the sky.
   d. from a transmitter to a receiver.
   e. directly through the ground.

3. Radio waves are said to be
   a. static.
   b. non-static.
   c. electromagnetic.
   d. ion free.
   e. weak.

4. Radio waves arise from the presence of rapidly alternating
   a. currents in the transmitter.
   b. currents in the transmitter's antenna.
   c. currents in the receiver.
   d. currents in the receiver's antenna.
   e. ion particles in the atmosphere.

5. Radio waves travel through the ether at
   a. 186,000 miles per hour.   d. both a & c.
   b. 186,000 miles per second.   e. b and/or c.
   c. the speed of light.

6. The layers of "electricity" high above the earth vary in altitude from
   a. 600 to 1,000 miles.   d. 600,000 to 750,000 feet.
   b. 300 to 750 miles.   e. 40 to 300 miles.
   c. 60 to 250 miles.

7. According to the article, long-range communications rely upon
   a. good telephone service.   d. the ground wave.
   b. better connectors.   e. non-jamming practices.
   c. the sky wave.

8. The upper region of the atmosphere consists of electrically charged particles
   a. originally emitted by the sun.   d. originally part of the moon.
   b. having like poles.   e. originally part of the planet Mars.
   c. visible only rarely.

9. The above mentioned charged particles are called
   a. strata-fibers.   d. "mirrors."
   b. stardust.   e. ions.
   c. atoms.

10. The ionosphere might most accurately be described as
    a. a sort of mirror.   d. a fence.
    b. a sieve.   e. an umbrella.
    c. a grate.

11. Over that portion of the earth where the sun's rays strike nearly vertically, openings in the ionosphere are
    a. large.   d. enlarged.
    b. small.   e. pear-shaped.
    c. non-existent.

12. "Radio waves are literally bounced off this 'mirror'." This statement is
    a. not accurate.   d. very accurate.
    b. accurate.   e. a half-truth.
    c. partially true.

13. When radio waves are not reflected, they
    a. go through large openings.   d. gain power.
    b. become weakened.   e. pass through the mesh and are lost
    c. are lost in space.   in space.

14. Openings in the electrical field in the ionosphere
    a. never vary in size.   d. are constant in size and in form.
    b. change in size frequently.   e. change even from minute to minute.
    c. are all pear-shaped.

15. The electrical ionosphere is created by
    a. the solar-plexus.   d. the sun.
    b. the solar time-year.   e. the moon.
    c. photostatic activity.

16. Engineers have ascertained this layer's presence by
    a. "dead-reckoning."   d. sending up radio pulses.
    b. electromagnets.   e. measuring light intensity.
    c. studying charts.

17. On the side of the earth exposed to the sun, the radio ceiling is
    a. much lower.
    b. much higher.
    c. average.
    d. twice as high as on the dark side.
    e. somewhat higher.

18. For night-time radio transmission, which frequencies are best?
    a. the higher ones.
    b. the lower ones.
    c. the medium ones.
    d. the very high ones
    e. the ultra-high ones.

19. Radio reception is usually better in the
    a. summer.
    b. spring.
    c. fall.
    d. winter.
    e. in-between seasons.

20. The sun is described as
    a. never changing.
    b. "a golden ball."
    c. changing seasonally.
    d. seldom changing.
    e. constantly changing.

21. The "dark spots" on the sun's surface are called
    a. dark spots.
    b. cyclonic disturbances.
    c. volcanos.
    d. sunspots.
    e. storm clouds.

22. The estimated temperature of the "dark spots" is
    a. 60,000° centigrade.
    b. 16,000° centigrade.
    c. 4,000° centigrade.
    d. 2,000° centigrade.
    e. 6,000° Fahrenheit.

23. The "dark spots" are believed to be
    a. storm areas.
    b. cooler than others.
    c. optical illusions.
    d. cyclonic low pressure areas.
    e. a, b, and d.

24. Their duration is normally
    a. eleven years.
    b. fourteen days.
    c. two years.
    d. two months.
    e. one week.

25. The sun's effect on radio communications affects mainly
    a. FM radio.
    b. television.
    c. AM radio.
    d. long-range reception.
    e. short-range reception.

Make certain that you've attempted all 25 questions, then check your answers with the Key for Inventory 1 inside the back cover. Deduct 4 points from 100 for each incorrect response, and record your comprehension score below.

Inventory Text 1: Comprehension Score: _____%

Selection 2 is to be read following the same procedure as that used for Selection 1.

Select a starting time and write it below.

Starting Time: MINUTES _____ SECONDS _____

As the second hand reaches the time you have written down, begin reading.

INVENTORY SELECTION 2

NARRATIVE OF A. GORDON PYM

by Edgar Allan Poe

Chapter 23

(Excerpt)

During the six or seven days immediately following we remained in our hiding place upon the hill, going out only occasionally, and then with the greatest precaution, for water and filberts. We had made a kind of penthouse on the platform, furnishing it with a bed of dry leaves, and placing in it three large flat stones, which served us for both fireplace and table. We kindled a fire without difficulty by rubbing two pieces of dry wood together, the one soft, the other hard. The bird we had taken in such good season proved excellent eating, although somewhat tough. It was not an oceanic fowl, but a species of bittern, with jet black and grizzly plumage, and diminutive wings in proportion to its bulk. We afterward saw three of the same kind in the vicinity of the ravine, apparently seeking for the one we had captured; but, as they never alighted, we had no opportunity of catching them.

As long as this fowl lasted we suffered nothing from our situation, but it was now entirely consumed, and it became absolutely necessary that we should look out for provision. The filberts would not satisfy the cravings of hunger, afflicting us, too, with severe gripings of the bowels, and, if freely indulged in, with violent headache. We had seen several large tortoises near the sea-shore to the eastward of the hill, and perceived they might be easily taken, if we could get at them without the observation of the natives. It was resolved, therefore, to make an attempt at descending.

We commenced by going down the southern declivity, which seemed to offer the fewest difficulties, but had not proceeded a hundred years before (as we had anticipated from appearances on the hilltop) our progress was entirely arrested by a branch of the gorge in which our companions had perished. We now passed along the edge of this for about a quarter of a mile, when we were again stopped by a precipice of immense depth, and, not being able to make our way along the brink of it, we were forced to retrace our steps by the main ravine.

We now pushed over to the eastward, but with precisely similar fortune. After an hour's scramble, at the risk of breaking our necks, we discovered that we had merely descended into a vast pit of black granite, with fine dust at the bottom, and whence the only egress was by the rugged path in which we had come down. Toiling again up this path, we now tried the northern edge of the hill. Here we were obliged to use the greatest possible caution in our manoeuvres, as the least indiscretion would expose us to the full view of the savages in the village. We crawled along, therefore, on our hands and knees, and, occasionally, were even forced to throw ourselves at full length, dragging our bodies along by means of the shrubbery. In this careful manner we had proceeded but a little way, when we arrived at a chasm far deeper than any we had yet seen, and leading directly into the main gorge. Thus our fears were fully confirmed, we found ourselves cut off entirely from access to the world below. Thoroughly exhausted by our exertions, we made the best of our way back to the platform, and, throwing ourselves upon the bed of leaves, slept sweetly and soundly for some hours.

For several days after this fruitless search we were occupied in exploring every part of the summit of the hill, in order to inform ourselves of its actual resources. We found that it would afford us no food, with the exception of the unwholesome filberts, and a rank species of scurvy-grass, which grew in a little patch of not more than four rods square, and would soon be exhausted. On the fifteenth of February, as near as I can remember, there was not a blade of this left, and the nuts were growing scarce; our situation, therefore, could hardly be more lamentable. On the sixteenth we again went round the walls of our prison, in hope of finding some avenue of escape; but to no purpose. We also descended the chasm in which we had been overwhelmed, with the faint expectation of discovering, through this channel, some opening to the main ravine. Here, too, we were disappointed, although we found and brought up with us a musket.

On the seventeenth we set out with the determination of examining more thoroughly the chasm of black granite into which we had made our way in the first search. We remembered that one of the fissures in the sides of this pit had been but partially looked into, and we were anxious to explore it, although with no expectation of discovering here any opening.

We found no great difficulty in reaching the bottom of the hollow as before, and were now sufficiently calm to survey it with some attention. It was, indeed, one of the most singular-looking places imaginable, and we could scarcely bring ourselves to believe it altogether the work of nature. The pit, from its eastern to its western extremity, was about five hundred yards in length, when all its windings were threaded; the distance from east to west in a straight line not being more (I should suppose, having no means of accurate examination) than forty or fifty yards. Upon first descending into the chasm—that is to say, for a hundred feet downward from the summit of the hill, the sides of the abyss bore little resemblance to each other, and, apparently, had at no time been connected, the one surface being of the soapstone, and the other of marl, granulated with some metallic matter. The average breadth or interval between the two cliffs was probably here sixty feet, but there seemed to be no regularity of formation. Passing down, however, beyond the limit spoken of, the interval rapidly contracted, and the sides began to run parallel, although, for some distance farther, they were still dissimilar in their material and form of surface. Upon arriving within fifty feet of the bottom, a perfect regularity commenced. The sides were now entirely uniform in substance, in color, and in lateral direction, the material being a very black and shining granite, and the distance between the two sides, at all points, facing each other, exactly twenty yards. The precise formation of the chasm will be best understood by means of a delineation taken upon the spot; for I had luckily with me a pocket-book and pencil, which I preserved with great care through a long series of subsequent adventures, and to which I am indebted for memoranda of many subjects which would otherwise have been crowded from my remembrance.

Stop. Note exact time and write it in below.

Finishing Time: MINUTES ———— SECONDS ————

Compute your reading rate of words per minute and write in below. This selection contains 1,140 words.

Selection 2: Reading Rate: ———— w.p.m.

Take the test, circling the letter before the most nearly correct answer.

INVENTORY COMPREHENSION TEST 2

1. From their hiding place on the hill, Pym and his companion went out for
    a. water and wood.
    b. water and fish.
    c. fish and wood.
    d. water and meat.
    e. water and filberts.

2. The platform on which they hid was referred to as
    a. a stone cliff.
    b. a treehouse.
    c. a jungle den.
    d. a penthouse.
    e. a magic carpet.

3. They kindled a fire by
    a. striking wet matches.
    b. striking two stones together.
    c. rubbing two pieces of dry wood together.
    d. rubbing a stone firmly on dry wood.
    e. rubbing two hard sticks together.

4. The bird which they ate was
    a. a raven.
    b. a species of bittern.
    c. a species of hawk.
    d. a type of bat.
    e. one of a group of long-legged crane.

5. The filberts, if freely eaten, caused
    a. a loss of vision.
    b. intense indigestion.
    c. great thirst.
    d. extreme dizziness.
    e. violent headaches.

6. The men left their hiding place later in search of
    a. water.
    b. snails.
    c. tortoises.
    d. birds which were to be cooked for food.
    e. seagull eggs.

7. They were hiding from
    a. the storms of life.
    b. themselves.
    c. savages in the village.
    d. the sheriff.
    e. the truant officer from their school.

8. To avoid being seen, they
    a. crawled on hands and knees.
    b. planted a decoy.
    c. took off their shirts.
    d. decided not to move.
    e. waited for nightfall before moving.

9. Returning to their starting point, they threw themselves upon
   a. the mercy of the court.
   b. a bed of straw.
   c. a pile of stones.
   d. a bed of ants.
   e. a bed of leaves.

10. This search is described as
    a. rewarding.
    b. fruitless.
    c. tiring.
    d. partly successful.
    e. ending early.

11. The hilltop afforded food only in the form of filberts and
    a. Johnson grass.
    b. scurvy-grass.
    c. tomatoes.
    d. Bermuda grass.
    e. summer grass.

12. The above mentioned food was soon
    a. killed.
    b. spoiled.
    c. frozen.
    d. totally eaten.
    e. stolen.

13. While examining the chasm, they found
    a. fresh berries.
    b. a cannon ball.
    c. a brown bear.
    d. a sword.
    e. a musket.

14. The pit, from east to west, was about
    a. 200 feet long.
    b. 200 yards long.
    c. 500 feet long.
    d. 1,000 yards long.
    e. 500 yards long.

15. The pit is described by Pym as the
    a. darkest place on earth.
    b. coldest place he'd seen.
    c. deepest hole on earth.
    d. most singular-looking place imaginable.
    e. hottest place on earth.

16. The chasm was
    a. 100 yards deep.
    b. 500 feet deep.
    c. 1,000 feet deep.
    d. some depth not stated.
    e. 20 yards deep.

17. One to the other, the sides of the chasm bore
    a. little resemblance.
    b. a most striking resemblance.
    c. a remote resemblance.
    d. a most strange resemblance.
    e. no resemblance.

18. The sides of the abyss, apparently, had
    a. been once connected.
    b. at no time been connected.
    c. been severely eroded.
    d. encrusted large diamonds and other stones.
    e. the same texture.

19. Within fifty feet of the bottom,
    a. the walls grew colder.
    b. the walls grew warmer.
    c. the walls grew darker.
    d. a perfect regularity commenced.
    e. Pym grew ill.

20. Pym had with him
    a. a pocket-book.
    b. a fountain pen.
    c. a yardstick.
    d. a pencil.
    e. a pocket-book and pencil.

21. The adventurers were apparently having
    a. a lot of fun.   d. great hardships.
    b. a party.   e. a vacation.
    c. no difficulties.

22. The author of the story is
    a. Pope.   d. Pugh.
    b. Allen.   e. Edgars.
    c. Poe.

23. Pym's whole name was
    a. A. Glenn Pym.   d. A. Gordon Pymm.
    b. Gordon A. Pymm.   e. A. Gordon Pym.
    c. A. Pym Gordon.

24. The story's title identifies it as
    a. a short story.   d. a prose work.
    b. a narrative.   e. both a thriller and prose work.
    c. a thriller.

25. This reading is an excerpt from Chapter
    a. 25.   d. 23.
    b. 26.   e. 22.
    c. 28.

Make certain you have attempted all 25 questions, then check your answers with the Key for Inventory 2 inside the back cover. Deduct 4 points from 100 for each incorrect response, and record your comprehension score below.

Inventory Test 2, Comprehension Score: _____%

In this inventory, we have given you two selections on different difficulty levels—one on science, and another on fiction—so that you might get a more accurate idea of your present reading efficiency, both in speed and comprehension.

Now obtain an average speed from the two readings.
    Selection 1: Rate _____ w.p.m.
    Selection 2: Rate _____ w.p.m.
    Add and divide by 2. Present rate: _____ w.p.m.
Next, obtain your average comprehension score.
    Selection 1: Comprehension _____%
    Selection 2: Comprehension _____%
    Add and divide by 2. Present comprehension _____%.
To become an Accelerated Reader, you must at least triple your reading rate and improve comprehension. To determine the minimum goals you are going to achieve, multiply as below.
    3 times _____ (present w.p.m.) = _____
    Comprehension better than _____%
Now you see where you are rate and comprehension-wise, and the minimum goals you are striving to attain. You can and will attain these goals with a conscientious application of the techniques in Part III of this book.

How You Learned To Read Slowly

The individual reads at the basic rate he has been taught to read. This fact is important in understanding why the so-called "average" reader can seldom achieve a rate far in excess of his speech rate, which is normally about 150 words per minute.

On the average, English speaking persons talk at the rate of 125 to 150 words per minute. The late Franklin D. Roosevelt spoke at the rate of 135 words per minute in his famous radio fireside chats. Sixty second radio and television commercials usually contain 100 to a maximum of 150 words, depending upon whether they are "soft" or "hard" sell.

Speech rates are fairly well fixed by practice and custom. Unfortunately, the same is too often true of basic reading rates. Most "untrained" readers normally read between 125 to 250 words per minute. With wide and extensive reading practice through the years, some have increased their reading rates to perhaps 350 w.p.m. or slightly more, but it is not likely that they will ever read faster unless they deliberately work at increasing reading rates.

Why is reading rate and the speech rate so closely tied together? For the answer one needs to recall the primary grades of his educational experience and recount how he was taught to read.

There, he normally was first taught letters of the alphabet. How did the teacher check each student's progress? *Orally.* Each student is required to respond aloud. At this point the student can't be expected to prove his ability by taking a multiple-choice test!

Then, as the instruction proceeds, the student learns words and simple expressions and sentences. Still, all the reading response is oral.

When the student reaches a certain degree of proficiency, he is told to "read to himself." This he must do even if the teacher has to hold a hand over his mouth to keep the oftentimes frustrated student from uttering continuous sounds.

With most students, the transition is finally made, more or less. Then the teacher is proud of her success. . . . Billy is now reading silently . . . and at the same slow pace he used to read aloud. Everything is fine so far, but the sad part is that Billy isn't normally given the slightest hint that now since he doesn't have to read aloud, he might increase his reading speed—that he might start looking for word "pictures" or ideas rather than just continuing with his slow word-hunting; that "ideas" are the important benefits to be gained, and the purpose for reading—not words.

Generally, when Billy starts "reading to himself" satisfactorily, he receives little if any further instruction in reading, and may well finish elementary, junior high, and high school—maybe even some college—and still be reading essentially at the same poor rate he learned and used when he was first taught to read silently.

The Eyes Have It

Exactly what determines reading rate?

You may be surprised to learn that it is controlled and determined mainly by eye movements, or the lack of them. Putting it rather technically, *reading rate is controlled primarily by the deviations of fixations made per line of print.*

Studies show that the slower the reader, the more his eyes move as he struggles over the page.

Very poor readers may make as many or more stops per line as there are letters in the words in that line. Good readers may stop (fixate) only once every two or three words, taking larger "bites" of each line. Excellent readers seldom stop more than twice per line, and only once per line on the shorter line lengths.

Then it would seem that the quickest way to increase reading rate would be to cut down on eye movement. We'll have much to say and to show you about this later.

How much do you know about the function of your eyes in reading?

EYES ARE LIVING CAMERAS

The best way to understand the eyes' operations in reading is to compare them with a camera. As you know, in photography the object to be photographed must be caught perfectly still when the camera's shutter is open, or the result will be a blur on the film. To take sharp pictures, both the subject and camera must be completely still when the shutter snaps. (High speed cameras and improved film have now made it possible to photograph objects in motion, but still the blur will show if the equipment is not right for the job.)

The case is the same in reading. The eye can see well enough to read with accuracy and certainly only when the eye is still (fixated). When the eye is in motion across the printed line, words are blurred and no actual reading can be done. In fact, as far as productive reading is concerned, all eye movement is a waste—a waste of time, energy, and comprehension.

WHICH READER-PHOTOGRAPHER ARE YOU?

Look at the sentences below and study the eye stops or fixations of three different types of readers. Each eye stop is numbered above the letter or word. Where would you place yourself as a reader-photographer?

The very poor (slow) reader:

1 2 3 4	5 6 7	8 9 10 11	12 13 14 15	16 17
W h e n	y o u	r e a d	w o r d	b y

18 19 20 21	22 23 24	25 26 27 28 29	30 31 32 33 34 35 36 37
w o r d	y o u	w a s t e	v a l u a b l e

38 39 40 41.
t i m e.

The slow word-for-word reader:

1	2	3	4	5	6	7	8	9	10
When	you	read	word	by	word	you	waste	valuable	time.

The better-than-average reader:

	1		2	3		4			
When	you	read	word	by	word	you	waste	valuable	time.

The Accelerated Reader:

	1				2				
When	you	read	word	by	word	you	waste	valuable	time.

It is not difficult to see how much longer it would take the very poor reader to cover the same material as the slow low word-for-word reader, and so on.

You know that when you drive your car, you hope to catch all the traffic lights green. If you do, all other conditions being equal, you'll arrive at your destination more refreshed and much sooner than if many or most lights were red. The same principle applies almost exactly to reading. Make fewer stops, and you get through sooner, and with better understanding of what you have read.

The Rewards of Accelerated Reading

A person's time is more or less valuable according to what is or can be accomplished. Naturally, the biggest reward of Accelerated Reading would be the conservation of time through greater achievement in the same amount of time; this greater achievement is the result of a fuller comprehension of what is read.

SPEED IMPROVES COMPREHENSION

When you learn to read faster, you'll better understand the meaning of what you read.

As a member in good standing of a slogan conscious society, you may be somewhat skeptical of such a statement. You no doubt believe in the often repeated sayings: "Haste makes waste," "The hurrieder I go, the behinder I get," and "Slow but steady wins the race," etc. If you do adhere to these slogans, now is the time to make a definite step toward progress—forget them!

While these "good old sayings" might apply well to some things, they have absolutely no claim to authority or truth in reading. The fact, proven again and again, is that when you learn to read faster, you'll have a more complete understanding of what you read. There are some important and provable reasons why this is true.

ACCELERATED READING REDUCES FATIGUE

How long does it now take you to read a novel of about 100,000 words? If you read at the rate of 200 words per minute, it takes approximately 8½ hours. For most slow readers, reading is just about as fatiguing as digging a ditch. How tired would you be after reading for 8½ hours? Likely your eyes would ache, your neck would be stiff, your back would feel broken, and you'd just about be ready for some sort of rest cure. Then is it not natural for slow readers to dread reading, and to shun as much of it as they can? Not many persons would have either the patience or time to sit for the full reading of such a novel; they would have to break frequently, and would not finish the book for a period of several days, or even weeks.

When you triple your reading rate, you'll be able to read that same 100,000 word novel in one-third the time! Your total reading time would be reduced from 8½ hours to about 2 hours and 45 minutes, saving approximately 5½ hours over your previous reading time. A person who reads only ten books a year could actually save over 50 hours reading time—that's more than a full work week!

The fact that faster reading gets the work done sooner naturally reduces the time required for reading, which results in a reduction of mental and physical fatigue. Comprehension is improved because the reader can concentrate more on what he is reading and less on his physical aches and pains which will result from prolonged periods of little physical activity and the tensions of reading.

ACCELERATED READING MAKES FOR COMPLETENESS OF THOUGHT

Do you think you'd really enjoy or get very much appreciation from seeing 15 minutes of a good movie today, leaving at the end of a scene, and returning tomorrow or the next day at the beginning of the next scene for another

15 minutes, and repeating this process until you had seen the entire film? If you did see the final segment two or three weeks later, do you think you would have satisfactorily captured the whole story, mood, theme, and meaning of the picture? Not likely. Yet, we expect to get complete meaning and appreciation from reading done in much the same tiresome way. We read Chapter One today, skip tomorrow, read Chapter Two the next day . . . so that we finally finish the book a week or two, or month later. Oftentimes we feel let down, confused, uncertain about the plot, the characters, and the purpose of the book. Well, what else should we expect?

Why do we stretch out readings over such extended periods? Mainly because few of us have many days when we can devote several hours to reading. Secondly, because it is too fatiguing and boring for most of us to read over an hour or so at one sitting, as was mentioned earlier. Also, whether we like to admit it or not, we do have one-track minds.

Now, maybe *you* don't have this one-track problem. That old saying about "one-track minds" is normally used as a joke, but it isn't really. We do have a spatial concept of time—sixty seconds to the minute, sixty minutes to the hour, twenty-four hours to the day, and so on. Our conscious mind runs along this track and does or thinks about only one thing at the time—that is, if anything is being thought of in a constructive manner. It is totally impossible to think with any efficiency about two or more things simultaneously.

Hopefully we think about what it is we're reading. If our mind wanders, we are, at that moment, thinking about something else entirely, and we will comprehend little of what's before us. We do, whether we like to admit it or not, have one-track minds.

Have you had to re-read relatively easy paragraphs, pages, or even entire chapters to get any meaning from them? If so, your whole attention was not on what you were reading the first time. Your one-track mind was, as we say, "out hunting rabbits."

Why was your mind wandering? You might give a dozen reasons, but most of them would, in final analysis, equal *boredom*—boredom resulting from slow, poorly motivated reading. And slow reading of the material hinders your ability to grasp the concept of what's being read in its entirety. As you read today, you are fervently trying to fit the pieces together—bits from yesterday's reading, and the day before, and maybe even a few pieces from last week's reading. It is a frustrating and frequently defeating task. For example, suppose you are reading a mystery in which you are introduced to a minor character, Aunt Mary, in Chapter One. She does not reappear again until the final chapter which you read several days later. To your chagrin, you discover that she holds a key position to other characters and to your understanding of the story and the mystery's solution—and you do not even remember that such a character ever appeared in the story at all.

A novel such as the one mentioned above can normally be read by the Accelerated Reader in one hour or less. If you had "met" Aunt Mary only an hour or so ago, you'd have a much better chance of remembering her vividly, and you would be able to weave her successfully into the plot and, consequently, get a better understanding of the whole story.

Certainly, developing the ability to complete most of your individual reading tasks in one or two sittings will greatly improve understanding and completeness of thought.

Most reading is something like fitting together a jigsaw puzzle. The bigger the pieces, the faster they fit together to form the whole picture. You can profit by developing the ability to read larger visual "bites" so that you may digest the material more completely.

Part II: Identify and Overcome Your Blocks to Better Reading

In a nutshell, *to read faster, you must overcome slow, ineffective reading habits.* Just to identify and overcome them, however, is not enough. They must be replaced with faster and more effective habits and practices. That is the two-fold purpose of this book.

While working closely with thousands of students studying to become Accelerated Readers, we have found that slow and ineffective reading is caused mainly by all, or a combination of some, six "blocks" which stood in the way of their reading faster and understanding better. You may not be hindered by all of these blocks, but it is important for your progress that you know what they are, and how to remove those which do stand in your way.

An explanation of each of the six blocks follows, as well as suggestions for removing them. Read carefully through and work on those which are your individual "demons." Identifying and understanding them will aid you very directly when you get to actual practice exercises later in this book.

Block 1—Failure to Preview

You wouldn't start on a vacation to a distant and unfamiliar place without a road map. You wouldn't dive into a pool without knowing the water's depth. You wouldn't attempt to cook a totally new dish without a recipe. Of course not!

But, would you be guilty of starting the reading of a book, a chapter, or a report without too much preparation or forethought? You may answer that you certainly wouldn't, but we'd have to disagree. We have found that most readers dive right into the business of reading with little if any preparation for, or idea of, what they are supposed to get from the experience.

How dare we disagree with your answer? Here's why. Every student who has taken our in-resident rapid reading course has served in a little experiment to see if they knew how to study effectively.

Early in the course they are given a history book and told that they have been assigned Chapter 10 for tomorrow's class. They are instructed to proceed with studying the chapter just as if they were at home or in study period.

Five minutes later they are asked to close the book and are given this test:
1. What is the chapter's title?
2. What is the author's name?
3. How many pages in the chapter?

4. How much time will you require to study this assignment?
5. Are there sub-headings in the chapter?
6. Are there any graphics in it?
7. Is there a formal summary or conclusion?
8. Are there study questions at the end?

Ninety-eight percent of them fail this simple test! Eight out of ten can answer only two or three questions! In brief, the results are catastrophic. Conclusion: Most individuals either don't know, or fail to use the few simple steps of preview (pre-reading) which would enable them to get the most benefit from the time spent reading the material.

Therefore, it may be well worth your time here to review the steps necessary for properly previewing different types of reading. Pre-reading can help you cut down your actual reading load by helping you to quickly determine whether what you have before you is worth spending the time to read thoroughly.

HOW TO PREVIEW A NON-FICTION BOOK

This is essentially the same procedure you were asked to follow before you began serious reading of this book:

1. Examine the outside—front and back. (Study title, illustrations; read the "blurbs" or comments on the jacket or cover; study the message on the end flaps, if any.)
2. Note the author's name and read any biographical information about him. What are his qualifications?
3. Check the publisher's name and the copyright date. (Dates are of utmost importance in many areas of study. The book, if unrevised, could be outdated. Study the publishing history—numbers and dates of reprints, revisions, etc. This information is normally to be found on back of the title page.)
4. Read the front matter—Introduction, Preface, Foreword, etc. (A quick check of this matter will give you a good idea of what the writer sets out to do in the book.)
5. Carefully look over the Table of Contents. (This is the skeletal out-line for the entire book. It will indicate the writer's approach and general treatment of the subject, the number of chapters, and their approximate length. It will also tip you off as to the back matter in the book—Indexes, Bibliographies, Glossaries, etc.)
6. Thumb through the book. (Stop briefly to note layout and typography. Briefly check any graphics—photographic inclusions, maps, charts, cartoons, graphs, etc.)
7. If there is an overall Summary or Conclusion, read it carefully.
8. Quickly look over Indexes or Glossaries if any are included.
9. Evaluate from your preview the book's value for your purpose.
10. Now you are ready to read with a purpose, or to select another title.

At first, this may seem like a lot of useless work and effort. On the contrary, it will take only a very few minutes—and these few minutes could well be the most important ones of your total time spent in study of the book.

HOW TO PREVIEW A BOOK OF FICTION

Since one of the principal motivating factors for reading fiction is to find out how the story ends, previewing a book of fiction should normally not include an attempt to "see how it turns out." However, your preview should include finding out as much about the book and its author as possible before you start to read. Read all the information printed on the outside of the book; find out all you can about the author; check the publisher and the copyright; read any front matter; look over the Table of Contents; thumb through the book; check the back matter (if any); evaluate it for your purpose and begin reading, or select another title.

HOW TO PREVIEW A CHAPTER

Most reading tasks in work and school or college involve the study and reading of portions—chapters, sections, parts—of books and other longer publications. The procedure for previewing parts of longer readings is essentially the same as previewing entire books, with a few variations:

1. Study the title. (In non-fiction it normally states in a very few words what is to be covered in the chapter.)
2. Question the title.
   a. What do I already know about this subject?
   b. Will this be review, or will it contain a lot of new information?
   c. What are the logical points to look for as I read?
   d. What will be the writer's attitude and approach?
   e. Does the title suggest his final conclusions?
   (This questioning technique helps to get your mind subject-oriented. It, in effect, prepares the thought soil for the seeds the writer has ready to plant in your field of knowledge.)
3. Count the pages. (Always make it a practice to know the approximate length of whatever you are going to read. You'll be better able to budget your reading and study time.)
4. Read the first paragraph or so. (These are usually introductory to the chapter's content.)
5. Next, read the *last* paragraph. (If there is no formal summary, the last paragraph usually summarizes.)
6. If there is a summary or conclusion, read it carefully. (It will tell you the main points to look for when you read the text.)
7. Look over any study questions or problems at the end. (They will aid you in guiding your study emphasis.)
8. Quickly page through the chapter. (Stop briefly to check graphics and sub-headings.)

9. Take a few moments to reflect upon what you have learned already, and what you expect to get from a careful study of the chapter.
10. You are now ready to read with a purpose, and you are prepared for better understanding of what you read.

Again, this may seem like a lot of effort to expend before actual reading, but rest assured the rewards in comprehension and total time gained are more than worth every one of the short moments required for an adequate preview of a chapter.

HOW TO PREVIEW A REPORT

Your desk may be piled high with reports which you wish you could get out of the way in the briefest time possible. You'll find that if you utilize a method of previewing them that is similar to the one you use in studying a book, they will vanish a lot faster than they do now. Of course, modifications are necessary for certain exceptional reports, but generally you should follow this questioning procedure:

1. Check the title. (What's the report about?)
2. Note the writer, his company, his department, etc. (Who prepared it?)
3. Review the date. (When was it prepared and written?)
4. Carefully note for whom it was prepared—person, company, department. (Was it prepared for me and my company?)
5. Read and understand the purposes and reasons for its preparation. (What's it supposed to prove or show?)
6. Study its Table of Contents or equivalent. (What is covered in the report?)
7. Read the Summary or Abstract carefully. (What are the final general conclusions and proposals, if any?)
8. Peruse all front and back matter. (What are the sources for the information contained in the report?)
9. Thumb through for sub-headings, organization, and typography. Study all graphs, charts, etc. (How is the report put together?)
10. Read as necessary.

HOW TO PREVIEW LETTERS

You may read hundreds or thousands of letters each year. You may find in many cases that this more rapid pre-reading may suffice for a great number of the more routine letters and communications that you now labor through. Read letters with these three steps in mind, *and in the suggested order:*

1. Check the top. (Letterhead, date, salutation.)
2. Check the bottom. (Writer's name and title.)
3. Check the middle for the main idea(s). (In most letters, you'll find the "meat" in or near the visual center. The first paragraph or so are

usually routine introduction and polite remarks. The last paragraph or so usually contains formalities.)

HOW TO PREVIEW MAGAZINE ARTICLES

In our rapidly changing world, magazines and other periodicals provide a convenient vehicle as a means of keeping abreast of what's happening in modern research and development. Consequently, the well-read individual must read several magazines and other publications each month. Utilize these simple steps to make magazine-type reading much faster and more rewarding.

1. Read the title and any sub-headings. (You'll get the general idea of the subject and its treatment.)
2. Check the writer's name and read any biographical notes about him.)
3. Carefully examine all graphics.
4. Read the first few paragraphs for the theme, etc.
5. Now read the first, or topic, sentence of all succeeding paragraphs.
6. Near the end of the article start reading more carefully when you sense the writer is giving his conclusions.

In this brief time you will know if the article is worth re-reading more carefully; if it is, the good skeletal framework you have formed will make your second reading mainly a review.

It is possible to see that previewing or pre-reading is an absolute necessity. It is certainly to your advantage to find out all you can about what you read before you invest a lot of your valuable time. Your preview will often prove that many of the things you now spend a lot of time laboring through do not even need to be read carefully—they contain no new or useful information, or they are only cleverly disguised sales letters concerning something you don't need, or they should be directed to another's attention entirely.

While previewing or pre-reading is not rapid reading *per se*, the practice can help you save enough time to make you feel that you are already an Accelerated Reader.

Use pre-reading with *everything* you read!

Block 2–Wasted Eye Movement

Have you ever observed the average reader's eyes as he reads? You'd notice that they tend to move across the line of print in a series of short jerks, stopping approximately once for each word. If you watch long enough, you'd notice that this jerky movement is frequently interrupted by glances above, below, to the sides, and even totally away from the page. These movements are known respectively as *regressions* (looking back, or above), *progressions* (looking ahead, or below), and *distractions* (looking totally away).

You'd also note that the eyes travel to the last printed word on the right, and then snap back to or into the left margin, much as the carriage returns to the left margin on an automatic electric typewriter.

Noting the Accelerated Reader, however, you'd see marked differences in the number and types of eye stops and movements. First, you'd note there are far fewer jerks. The eyes move across the line in two or three stops. (And remember that reading rate is determined to a large degree by the number of stops the eyes make while reading a line—the fewer stops, the faster the rate.)

Further, you'd note that the left-right swing of the eyes would include actual travel over only one-half the total line length, and that this half is over the second and third quarters of each line. The eyes do not move over the first nor fourth quarters of the line.

Also, you'd note few if any regressions, progressions, and certainly a bare minimum of visual distractions.

Incidentally, you'd notice that he was turning the pages a lot faster, too!

MINIMIZING REGRESSIONS

The most effective means for overcoming the wasteful habit of looking back to see what you missed the first time is simply to stop doing it. It will help you to stop if you realize that the benefit gained by regressing is seldom worth the time required.

Try to develop this attitude: If I didn't get some little point the first time, I'll get it straight and in proper order when I read through the material again. Senseless? Not at all. When you learn to preview thoroughly, and practice so that you are reading at least three times faster than you now read, you'll have created a built-in review. In other words, you can, if necessary, read the material *three* times in the same amount of time you once required to read it through only one time! In addition, when you re-read, you can employ spatial (spaced out) study which many educators favor for deep and thorough learning. This simply means that you can read the material again later in the day, or tomorrow, or later. It is the same general process you probably use to prepare for examinations; you know it as review.

In reading, the only profitable direction for the eyes to move is forward—down the page. To aid you at first in overcoming regressions, we suggest that you slide a blank card or piece of paper down the page, covering each line as it is read. This way you can't look back to re-read.

It is emphasized that this is to be done only *temporarily*. The practice should not be continued for any extended period. In actual rapid reading, the entire page must be totally exposed to the eye and mind. Furthermore, the mechanics of manually covering portions of the page would be cumbersome and too time-consuming.

You'll have extensive practice in overcoming regressions later in this book.

MINIMIZING PROGRESSIONS

The reader who is constantly noting the number at the bottom of the page, checking out unusual words or visual patterns caused by certain combinations of printed letters on the page, or even flipping over a page or so to see how many more pages have to be waded through, simply is not thinking very effectively about what he is reading. His mind is too often elsewhere.

When inattention and impatience become too great, it is best to simply put the book aside until such time as you are psychologically prepared to devote the attention which the reading deserves and demands for satisfactory comprehension.

At the risk of appearing ridiculously over-simple, we must say that the best way to overcome time- and comprehension-wasting progressions is just to stop the practice.

Minimizing the practice of constantly looking ahead will be facilitated greatly by adequately previewing the material. In your pre-reading, quickly check through the whole assignment before you begin intensive study. Then you'll *know* how many pages are in the reading. You'll *know* the approximate amount of time you'll require for reading. You'll *know* what the charts, graphs, maps, etc., are about, and you won't have to interrupt your reading to study them. And most important, your preview, if properly done, will help to stimulate your interest so that it will be easier to keep your mind on the subject in general, and specifically on the paragraph being read at the moment.

In short, to minimize progressions make a thorough preview of the material to be read, as discussed earlier in this book.

MINIMIZING DISTRACTIONS

When the eyes are moved totally off the page, it is natural to assume that the mind is moved totally away from the subject at hand.

What has been said about minimizing regressions and progressions applies as well to minimizing distractions. Maintain a constant vigilance to see that you make a *business* of your reading; save the distractions for a time when you can enjoy them.

The devastating effects of distractions can be minimized by observing a few common sense rules of the "how and why" of studying.

Generally speaking, before you begin to read, make a few definite preparations for reading. You make preparations for a bath, don't you? Go to your "reading place"—your desk, your room, the kitchen table . . . a place where you can be reasonably comfortable. Get away from the television set, and out of the mainstream of activity. Clear the area of all reading and study materials except those you actually need at the moment. Concentrate light on your desk or book; if possible, have another soft light on in the room. Make sure the area isn't too warm—you might get drowsy. And don't study too long without rewarding yourself with a break.

When do you break? Take a breather when you start finding it difficult to keep your attention on what you are reading. When you do break, get physically as well as mentally away from your reading materials. You might take a short walk through the house or office, get a cup of coffee, or eat something. In a few minutes you should be able to return and resume your effective reading and study.

Block 3–Poor Vision Span

As stated several times previously in this book, but important enough to repeat, the average reader tends to move his eyes across the page and the printed line in a series of short jerks, stopping approximately once per word. And again, to read faster, the number of eye stops, or eye fixations, must be reduced. Any reduction, however minor, will tend to increase reading rate. With a realistic increase in rate, better comprehension can be expected to follow.

In order to reduce the number of stops, it is necessary to train the eyes to pay conscious attention to a larger area of the page with each fixation. This is called by some developing the peripheral, or side, vision. Untrained, we tend to pay conscious, or reading, attention to only 5 to 10 percent of our total visual area. It is not plausible to assume that we could ever develop the ability to use the total vision area for actual reading, but it is credible to assume that this reading area can be enlarged, or more of it utilized, through a conscientiously applied series of drills designed to offer practice in seeing wider areas around a fixed point.

It is indeed practically possible to enlarge this area, to increase the vision span, to develop or utilize more of the so-called "side vision." A case in point is the well developed side vision of a good basketball player. With increased practice on the court, he develops the ability to see what is going on on both sides of him with a very minimum amount of head and eye movement. This is necessary if he is to see where he is going with the ball and at the same time remain alert to the moves of his opponents.

This is another example of Nature's ability to enable us to adjust to the needs and demands of our environment. With patient practice, the eyes will adjust quickly to the need to see a larger area of the page each time they fixate.

Block 4–Vocalization and Sub-Vocalization

Sub-vocalization (reading aloud silently) has been discussed briefly in the section "How You Learned to Read Slowly," But it is certainly important that you understand what it is and how you may overcome it so that you may become an Accelerated Reader faster. As a matter of fact, until you do effectively reduce all vocalization during silent reading, your reading rate can never much exceed your speech rate of about 150 words per minute.

How will you know when you are vocalizing? Look at your reading rate which you determined earlier in this book. The closer it is to 150 or below, the stronger the proof that you are reading aloud, actually or figuratively, to yourself.

This carry-over from your early primary reading practice must be minimized as much and as soon as possible and, hopefully, in time totally eliminated.

"But," the average reader complains, "I can't understand what I read unless I do say the words as I read them." This argument sounds rational to many, but under a little analysis proves less so.

Recall your most recent shopping trip? Did you speak silently or aloud to yourself as you looked at all the merchandise, checked the price tags, and made selections? Not likely.

When you walk through a new home, is it not possible to observe with accuracy the furnishings and floor plan without speaking to your inner ear?

We constantly go about making visual observations, evaluations, and actual decisions without uttering a single word either outwardly or inwardly.

With practice, the average individual can learn to do the same with his reading. It should be mentioned, however, that when reading the English language, we are confronted with 26 different alphabetic symbols (letters) and ten numbers and, consequently, it takes a more careful and systematic method of observation to recognize the infinite letter combinations which form words than it would, say, to recognize an elephant as a distinct entity. Therefore, it is necessary to develop a regular and systematic means for covering the printed page thoroughly and adequately; this method will be dealt with in the Two-Stop pattern in Part III.

Reading rates near the speech rate—150 words per minute—are not the only symptoms of vocalization and sub-vocalization. To identify these other more or less overt signs, we have had (in some cases, in a humorous vein) to invent descriptive words or terms. These five additional signs of vocalization we have dubbed as follows: *lipping, tongue-warbling, jawing, Adam's-appling,* and *diaphragming.*

LIPPING

Slow readers always demonstrate excessive eye movement. In addition, many slow readers "lip-read" on one or more of three definite movement levels.

First, there is the slowest reader who speaks words aloud. Not only is lip movement obvious, but there is constant oral sound as well.

Second, there is the whisperer. He seldom utters vocal sounds, but normally limits himself to the audible whisper.

The above two "lippers" are easy to detect. And you'll have no difficulty in recognizing these time-consuming and limiting practices if you are guilty of utilizing them.

Number three, the "lip-sync-er," is harder to detect. He seldom, if ever, makes an audible sound while reading, but his lips are just as busy forming each sound as if he were actually reading aloud. Do you lip-sync? To find out, place a finger lightly on the lips as you read, or ask a friend to observe you as you read for several minutes. You may be surprised to find how busy your lips actually are.

In all the above cases, reading rate is literally anchored fast to the individual's speech rate. The only way the dyed-in-the-wool "lipper" will ever increase his reading rate is to learn to talk faster. And this has its drawbacks since he'd then have difficulty conversing.

These three "lipping" practices can be overcome quickly by first knowing that there is lip movement when you read, and then by applying these very simple suggestions if there is.

1. Cup your hands behind both ears as you read. If you hear any sounds or whispers at all, continue to listen until you break the habit.
2. Read with a pencil held lightly between the lips. Any movement of the lips will be pointed out and exaggerated by the movement of the pencil and will be easy to spot.
3. In severe or extreme cases, the mouth can be sealed temporarily with plastic tape.

A short period of reading practice with the remedies suggested here should completely eliminate "lipping" and move you up an important step on the ladder to Accelerated Reading.

TONGUE-WARBLING

Birds are said to warble and utter sweet sounds, but readers should not. The "tongue-warbler" is a near-master at concealing his practice. You'll have to watch his throat (under the chin) to catch him. Outwardly, his lips are usually as steady as those of the very best ventriloquist's, but his tongue is busily engaged in forming each and every sound.

As you read this paragraph, are you aware of even the slightest tongue movement? If so, you must overcome it, however slight it may be.

Good results in stopping "tongue-warbling" may be obtained by first becoming aware that it is going on, and then briefly trying these suggestions.

1. Read with a pencil gripped midway back in the mouth, with the tongue held underneath.
2. Read with chewing gum held between the top of the tongue and the roof of the mouth.

JAWING

The "jawer" does exactly what the term implies. His lower jaw keeps time with his reading. His lips often are completely sealed, but the jaw is still very much in motion. If you need to overcome this tiresome habit, try these.

1. Read with your chin resting on your clinched fist. The elbow is planted firmly on the table.
2. Read while chewing gum. But make certain that you don't chew in time with your reading.
3. Read with a pencil clinched firmly between the teeth.

ADAM'S-APPLING

We come next to the reader who has succeeded in ostensibly cutting out all external and internal head movement and has substituted throat exercises.

As he reads, unconsciously he puts his voice box and vocal cords through all the intricate adjustments for speaking. He raises and lowers pitch (inaudibly) as he experiences the action of the words he reads on the printed page. If a sensitive microphone were attached to the throat, he might be surprised to learn of all the "speaking" that is going on below his normal hearing level.

Check yourself now. Place your fingers lightly around your Adam's apple, or voice box. Any movement or vibration going on there except that which is necessary for breathing and swallowing? If so, you are "Adam's-appling." Put a stop to it with these hints.

1. Consciously and deliberately relax the entire throat.
2. Read with your fingers held lightly touching the voice box. Any vibration or movement will alert you to relax further until there is no "Adam's-appling" evident.

DIAPHRAGMING

The "diaphragmer" puts action into his silent reading by regulating his breath to correspond with the words and phrases as he reads. He is, in effect, projecting his silent speech. Aside from slowing down his reading rate, he may also find extended reading periods quite exhaustive.

To test yourself for this weakness in reading, place a finger beneath the nostrils to see if you detect any erratic breath action. Place the other hand on the stomach and see if the rhythm of your breathing corresponds directly to that of your reading.

Overcome this tiring practice by reading with your hands placed as suggested above until you note no direct connection of breath with your reading.

All of these vocalizing and sub-vocalizing practices can be overcome readily as soon as they are identified and effort is exerted to stop them.

Block 5—Miscellaneous Weaknesses

It is necessary to mention three other blocks to faster reading. While some of them may seem rather insignificant, they should nonetheless be identified and eliminated if any one or all of them hamper your progress.

The first of these is pointing or marking with a hand, pencil, ruler, card, or any other device. Do not point out your reading, ever. The page should be totally exposed to the eyes. If you can't resist pointing, put pens, pencils, etc., out of reach so that you won't unconsciously pick them up and start using them. If your fingers persist in returning to the page to "keep you from losing the place," actually sit on them until you learn to rely on your eyes to do the job of keeping your place.

Hand scanning, recommended by some exponents of rapid reading, is the second miscellaneous weakness to avoid. Any covering of the page for whatever purpose limits your chances for rapid and complete understanding of the material on that page. Any movement of a hand either down or across the page is distracting and hampers comprehension. Hand scanning is, in fact, a "crutch" and has no purpose in your program to increase reading rate and improve comprehension.

The third of these lesser blocks to rapid reading is improper page turning. Our observations of all types of readers prove that some ineffective readers may take an average of 4 seconds to turn a page and resume reading. This is nearly as much time as faster readers require to read the same page! At 4 seconds per page, the reading of a 400 page book would involve over 13 minutes of time wasted in page turning alone.

Ideally, a book should be printed in one long continuous sheet, but since there are no 500 foot bookshelves, this sheet is chopped into more convenient shorter sections called pages. Therefore, the thought does not necessarily end at the bottom of a page, but often continues on the next page, which should be presented to the eye and mind as quickly as possible for maximum comprehension.

For more efficiency in page turning, it is best to read with the book flat on a desk or table top. As soon as your eyes begin reading the top of the left hand page, feel out with the thumb and forefinger of the right hand the next single sheet. This will help you in avoiding the frustrating mistake of turning more than one sheet at a time. As soon as you finish reading the right hand page, flip the paper quickly, and, if necessary, use the fingertips of the left hand to hold down the newly turned page. Repeat the "feel-out" process immediately.

If the pages strongly resist lying flat as is often the case with soft-back titles, it might be advisable to "break" the book's back. This is accomplished by holding the book in both hands, and bending it forcibly and repeatedly all the way back so that the front and back covers touch. This breaking should be done about every 10 or 15 pages. This process relaxes the binding and if properly done, allows the pages to lie flat without the necessity of holdng them down by hand.

Part III: Become an Accelerated Reader

Now that you have studied the theory, and are well on the way toward overcoming the negative practices which have stood in your way to faster reading, it is time to show you the secrets which will help you to at least triple your speed and improve comprehension.

In Part III you'll be shown how to become the rapid reader you want to be. However, the fact that you are shown all the methods of the Accelerated Reading Method is no guarantee that you will give these exercises the necessary attention to actually achieve your goal. You know it is true that you can go to your physician and he can prescribe the proper medication for your malady, but he can't make you take it. It is, in the final analysis, up to the individual whether or not he is to be successful in whatever he sets out to achieve.

Learning to triple your reading rate is worth whatever amount of time it may require. You'll have mountains of reading to do in the future. Why not devote a little serious attention now to preparing yourself to successfully cope with all the reading you'll have to do in the years to come. We are betting on *you!*

In Part III, we shall practice to develop eye control, increase vision span, learn the Two-Stop Method, and practice to make perfect your newly improved skills.

Develop Eye Control and Expand Vision

In the exercises that follow, concentrate the eyes upon the *center* letter of each line. Then, without eye movement either to the left or the right, read aloud, or vocalize silently the letters in this order: *center* letter, *left* letter, *right* letter.

Then move the eyes straight down to the next line and repeat through the entire page of drill.

DRILL A

F	M	E
W	K	G
Q	J	N
S	V	B
P	G	J
A	E	N
R	G	Y
C	W	J
L	Q	C
V	R	Y
B	M	V
S	G	J
B	O	K
Q	T	L
X	U	I
S	K	D
M	P	E
K	J	G
C	T	L
E	J	G
A	K	M
W	U	P
M	U	G
B	H	G
S	C	K
V	K	E
W	J	M
O	T	J
J	A	L
E	M	V

The width of Drill A is about 1¼ inches—the area the average untrained reader can see well enough to read with a minimum effort.

If you experienced any difficulty the first time through, repeat Drill A several times. Pay close attention to your eyes so that you'll start becoming aware of undesired left-right movement. It might be helpful at first for you to recruit the services of a member of the family or a friend to watch your eyes as you practice for any left-right movement, and to caution you when you move in any direction but down the page. Soon, as you gain proficiency, you'll be able to quickly detect the slightest unwanted movement, and will be able to minimize it.

In repeating Drill A, and those drills following, you will find the letters easier to read if you focus slightly above the line of letters, rather than right in the middle of the letter itself. You'll find this is true in regular reading as well. Often the white spaces between words serve as white pickets on a fence that tend to hamper the eyes from going smoothly on to the next word. If you look slightly above the tops of the printed letters, your eyes will be moving in smooth, uninterrupted white space.

Don't force or strain to see while practicing. *Relax.* And it is very probable at this point that you will make numerous errors in calling all of the letters correctly. This is to be expected, and is all right at first. Of utmost importance now is *eye control*—having the eyes look where you direct them, rather than where habit would have them look. Your accuracy will improve as your vision span increases with practice.

Once you master Drill A, practice Drill B aloud or silently, calling the letters in this order: center, *immediate* left, *immediate* right, *far* left, *far* right.

DRILL B

L	CSB	K
M	YPD	V
E	PGL	M
X	GMI	P
C	RKG	L
W	CYH	P
E	DNL	Q
A	DJM	L
B	SKH	L
V	TKF	M
C	MRI	D
B	MRC	T
O	SLO	V
T	AMG	Y
O	PVB	J
W	MGI	L
B	KCD	W
K	GBN	R
B	AKT	J
V	MTO	L
W	GDI	X
R	UVD	Y
B	RPL	M
D	YFO	Z
T	NFI	U
J	LDN	M
E	OFN	P
D	IVN	D
W	KTP	B
P	IMV	Q

Notice: You'll find it more productive and less fatiguing if you work frequently for short periods of time on these drills rather than in one or two long sessions. It is normal for the eyes to feel a little "strange" or tire quickly at first, but this will diminish and will hardly be noticeable after a few practice sessions.

After Drill B is mastered, go on to Drill C, then Drill D, then E, mastering each before going to the next. All drills may be repeated as many times as necessary now, as well as from time to time throughout your reading improvement program.

Note when you get to Drill E that it has an overall width of 3¼ inches—the normal column width of most softback books. When you can do Drill E, you should be able to read straight down the center of a 3¼ inch column width of print without too much difficulty. However, most students are reluctant to spend the time necessary with the eye drills for such peripheral development and, though highly desirable, it is not absolutely necessary in order for you to at least triple your reading speed. We'll explain this further when we discuss the Two-Stop practice.

DRILL C

T	J	M	G	E
P	S	B	N	R
C	E	L	Y	K
X	D	W	A	Z
L	Y	V	D	C
K	P	W	A	X
X	G	W	K	M
Z	Y	I	P	M
W	D	X	B	M
Z	T	I	L	B
A	U	T	K	Y
V	M	S	R	K
K	T	D	X	C
Q̲	G	J	I	L
A̲	J	E	I	R
B	D	X	L	C
S	G	U	R	K
C	H	T	D	L
G	L	I	P	K
N	R	D	H	I
W	G	Q̲	K	P
J	Y	K̲	M	N
O	L	G	P	D
T	K	I	L	P
Z	D	T	U	L
Y	K	N	W	Z
U	M	D	S	C
S	H	K	T	L
B	D	R	F	E
H	I	L	M	P

DRILL D

V	U	SBN	E	L
S	I	CKR	S	L
X	R	DLT	C	Y
P	G	RKY	V	J
B	F	LDI	P	H
O	Y	SJR	J	T
I	G	LRI	D	P
F	G	SYT	J	W
R	T	RTL	C	S
Z	F	GLT	B	R
Q	D	GKY	L	G
Z	P	TIL	V	M
L	M	VYT	K	E
W	A	FKY	N	C
A	S	MSL	W	Z
Q	D	GKI	Z	B
N	I	OSD	L	W
P	L	WLT	D	F
T	G	BMN	S	T
B	R	BCN	X	K
P	J	SCB	W	L
S	G	YTR	I	H
K	H	YGT	G	V
I	H	RJF	H	B
X	G	UKV	F	H
A	X	BJT	T	U
D	B	RKT	V	S
M	B	FKR	K	L
O	C	VIJ	F	Y
S	K	TLY	C	Z

DRILL E

H	F	D	BAC	E	G	I
C	S	P	URL	N	B	N
M	D	R	TYH	B	M	S
L	S	K	DTB	X	J	W
L	A	D	RYM	C	K	E
P	A	F	GTW	Q	M	D
T	K	F	EXB	U	M	W
T	N	D	RWS	C	I	A
R	J	E	PQT	X	P	M
L	E	G	JWQ	U	I	N
S	J	D	VBN	Z	Q	T
M	E	O	IUK	L	A	P
L	B	W	SAI	F	B	C
F	T	Q	HLS	C	V	M
C	M	E	SBC	D	H	E
M	R	W	QUM	L	D	J
A	D	Q	GXB	M	K	L
R	E	S	SCN	F	S	D
L	B	D	TYZ	V	S	L
B	R	S	QUI	E	P	W
W	L	T	HKX	A	T	H
K	L	T	BZS	W	W	L
C	B	S	NBC	A	B	C
K	L	R	UZA	M	F	E
H	P	U	QUT	V	E	B
C	T	G	BMD	R	M	A
E	X	B	CDJ	F	H	Q
B	N	J	FWQ	T	P	M
M	S	F	ACH	R	M	S
P	Q	K	LSG	A	W	E

PRACTICAL APPLICATION

Newspaper and magazine columns provide excellent ground for practicing the eye control and vision expansion which you have been developing.

Before starting to practice news columnar reading, use a ruler or other straight-edge to trace a straight line down the very vertical center of several columns. Then make your eyes follow the line down while attempting to see all words on either side of the center. Repeat each column several times, noting that your comprehension improves with each repetition. It must be emphasized that neither speed nor good comprehension is the main objective here. Development of eye control and better "side vision" are the main goals. At first, as your eyes move down the columns, you'll have a tendency to scan left and right, but with practice this urge to do so will be minimized and in time overcome totally.

Very soon you should begin practice on narrow columns without the line down the middle. Be careful to control the eyes so that the only movement is down, not left, right, or up.

Several sessions of practice on Drills A through E, and newspaper and magazine columnar reading may be necessary to assure conscious control of the eyes. And this is important to remember: when you succeed in reducing the number of stops your eyes make on a page, you will reduce the amount of time required to read the page. As time is reduced, speed increases. As speed increases, comprehension improves.

Developing the ability to see wider areas is necessary to rapid reading, and so is developing the ability to see deeper areas. The drills which follow will aid you in developing a greater depth consciousness, as well as offering additional practice in expanding width.

In Drill F, focus on the italicized center letter, and read alternately left and right from the *inside* out. Make only one fixation to read the *two* lines together; then move down to the next group, etc. Repeat as necessary.
Notice: For alternate practice, this drill and all letter drills can be practiced by beginning at the bottom of the page and reading up.

When practicing Drill G, focus on the italicized letter in the center of each group of letters, and read from the inside out, alternately to the left and to the right. Do the same on Drills H, I, and J.

DRILL F

R	Z	M
G	A	T
E	I	H
C	O	M
A	I	T
Z	X	B
Z	O	I
W	T	O
Q	B	N
U	I	Y
V	T	O
S	B	A
J	N	K
B	R	T
R	M	P
Y	D	A
S	I	W
J	B	K
R	T	M
W	C	L
P	I	M
O	I	V
M	K	R
D	O	K
O	Z	S
J	M	W
I	T	M
E	B	S
T	I	B
R	W	V

DRILL G

A	R	NQT	B	D
C	K	AKP	N	R
M	D	YRL	X	A

K	D	LPY	K	S
M	F	KTP	B	X
R	O	LDH	M	R

K	Q	DMT	A	J
M	F	LDF	M	T
Y	M	FLP	B	C

O	F	KVM	T	P
V	K	XPR	O	S
D	P	MCO	F	K

I	E	SLT	B	H
O	C	HDU	L	S
C	P	FKY	R	N

J	R	UGJ	X	I
A	B	FKT	J	K
A	K	FTU	J	S

A	I	VRP	C	I
L	D	TPB	M	T
L	R	IDF	V	G

Q	L	JML	I	X
P	F	WPG	V	K
F	J	YPL	M	R

X	O	UML	V	N
Q	B	AMR	Z	O
F	L	NML	D	B

W	P	LVR	X	V
K	R	PFJ	R	L
C	O	ELX	A	I

DRILL H

R	M	Z	P	N
S	K	T	B	N
A	J	M	W	N
J	F	K	B	M
W	O	N	V	J
Q	I	B	A	L
F	B	E	I	C
P	F	M	V	L
J	F	B	K	D
S	L	N	I	E
L	S	M	A	T
K	D	M	W	P
A	L	T	B	T
Z	O	J	M	X
W	P	K	S	M
P	T	G	N	X
K	G	N	C	M
P	S	L	C	M
T	O	L	D	L
E	P	B	X	L
S	L	U	M	C
O	F	A	K	D
S	K	M	T	O
I	D	L	R	P
Q	M	Z	V	Y
K	C	Y	L	E
M	S	J	L	T
H	C	S	M	W
K	D	J	U	T
R	J	O	L	S

DRILL I

T	E	ESN	N	O
D	L	SCB	N	E
W	P	F*H*B	S	O
A	L	FCB	G	O
X	B	WYO	P	F
Q	O	PAB	C	M
E	K	GZS	F	A
L	S	HVN	T	I
D	I	EGB	P	D
W	L	QCX	O	K
K	R	DMG	Y	N
X	O	EJQ	O	L
A	Z	FWJ	P	K
B	J	KRS	E	L
P	A	TGB	R	V
D	U	KVX	Z	M
V	J	EOP	G	M
K	R	FXB	M	I
T	M	JRD	V	J
K	A	VUT	Y	B
A	K	DUR	I	H
G	Y	WLM	U	D
D	B	X*H*Y	J	N
T	N	FIV	F	L
R	P	HCW	Q	M
A	I	OMP	C	I
D	K	WQJ	K	I
L	S	F*H*Y	C	O
W	G	BJY	L	W
S	N	VXE	D	P

DRILL J

C	S	P	URL	N	B	N
M	D	R	TYH	B	M	S
L	S	K	DTB	X	J	W
L	A	D	RYM	C	K	E
P	A	F	GTW	Q	M	D
T	K	F	EXB	U	M	W
T	N	D	RWS	C	I	A
R	J	E	PQT	X	P	M
L	E	G	JWQ	U	I	N
S	J	D	VBN	Z	Q	T
M	E	O	IUK	L	A	P
L	B	W	SFB	C	X	C
F	T	Q	HLS	C	V	M
C	M	E	SBC	D	H	E
M	R	W	QUM	L	D	J
A	D	Q	GXB	M	K	L
R	E	S	SCN	F	S	D
L	B	D	TYZ	V	S	L
B	R	S	QUI	E	P	W
W	L	T	HKX	A	T	H
K	L	T	BZS	W	W	L
C	B	S	NBC	F	T	H
K	L	R	UZA	M	F	E
H	P	U	QUT	V	E	B
C	T	G	BMD	R	M	A
E	X	B	CDJ	F	H	Q
B	N	J	FWQ	T	P	M
M	S	F	ACH	R	M	S
P	Q	K	LSG	A	W	E
R	S	L	BSQ	T	Y	A

When you master Drills A through J with vocal and/or sub-vocal practice, do them again several times *without* vocalization of any kind. Focus on the center letter in each line and try to recognize all letters in each individual line, but without consciously repeating any single letter to yourself.

If you have a tendency to vocalize or sub-vocalize, you might count from 1 to 10 aloud, or recite some simple poem or the lyrics to a song you know well as your eyes visually comprehend each row of letters. This practice in "sight reading" aids in overcoming vocalization in reading, and increases rates.

Let us mention again that mastering the above drills is of utmost importance. They cannot be practiced too much; however, do not overdo your practice at any one time.

Pacing and Block Reading

Even with a larger and more effective vision area, beginner rapid readers are sometimes hindered from achieving exciting reading rates because of their reluctance to maintain an accelerated rate throughout a longer reading. Oftentimes they may get bogged down and lose ground in maintaining the word per minute rate of which they are capable.

The purpose of the following drills is to give you practice in pacing—maintaining a fairly regular and steady rate over a page. The drills are to be practiced without too much worry about comprehension. Try to become used to the rhythm as you count your way down and then up the page.

Drill K contains 30 rows of five letters each. Your focal point on each row is the center letter. Your eyes should move down, one row at a time, one fixation per line. Aloud, or to yourself, maintain a regular count from 1 to 30.

At first, only attempt to "sight read" the three inner columns. Practice moving also from bottom to top of the page.

When you master the inside three letters of each row, repeat the same process as you read all five columns. Remember that your eyes can see accurately enough to read only when they stop. If you see only a blur as you move down the page, you are scanning, or sweeping, in a continuous motion over the page. You *must* stop—briefly, but totally—on *every* line in this drill.

DRILL K

D	B	A	C	E
K	T	L	Y	C
C	V	I	J	F
V	F	K	R	K
B	R	K	T	V
X	B	J	T	T
G	U	K	V	F
H	R	J	F	H
H	Y	G	T	G
G	Y	T	R	I
J	S	C	B	W
R	B	C	N	X
G	B	M	N	S
R	B	C	N	X
J	S	C	B	W
G	Y	T	R	I
H	Y	G	T	G
A	R	J	F	H
G	U	K	V	F
X	B	J	T	O
B	R	K	T	V
V	F	K	R	K
C	V	I	J	F
K	T	L	Y	C
Z	U	B	R	L
Q	L	D	G	K
L	W	A	F	K
M	Z	V	G	P
L	S	G	Y	T
K	A	U	J	O

Now repeat Drill K, taking two lines with each fixation and move down the page for a count of 15. Your focal point will be *between* the center letters of each two lines. If you come out "uneven," continue to practice until you have seen all letters by the count of 15.

Then repeat Drill K, taking three lines with each fixation and move down the page for a count of 10. You may make this count a little slower at first. Practice several times until you come out "even."

The short article, Drill L, which follows is to be "sight read" in the same manner as you practiced Drill K. Focus in the center of the column, move down ONE line at a time, and count *aloud* or *silently* as you cover the entire reading. Do not vocalize any words in the selection. Repeat it one line at a time with counting as many times as necessary until you feel you totally understand the content.

Then repeat it at two lines per focus. Then repeat again at three lines per focus. Don't be concerned that you are repeating the same reading so many times. You are learning a technique of reading. Later you will apply it to your individual reading requirements, but you must first learn the methods thoroughly.

DRILL L

The Basic Idea

The basic idea of social security is a simple one: During working years, employees, their employers, and self-employed people pay social security contributions, which go into special funds; and when earnings stop or are reduced because the worker retires, dies, or becomes disabled, monthly cash benefits are paid from the funds to replace part of the earnings the family has lost.

Part of the contributions made during the working years go into a separate hospital insurance trust fund so that when workers or their dependents reach 65 they will have paid-up hospital insurance to help pay their hospital bills.

A program of supplementary medical insurance, which is available to people 65 or over, helps them pay doctors' bills and other medical expenses. This program is voluntary and, instead of being paid for out of social security contributions, is financed out of premiums shared half-and-half by the older people who sign up and the Federal Government.

Nine out of ten working people in the United States are now building protection for themselves and their families under the social security program.

The successful Accelerated Reader is able to read in "blocks" or large "bites" of the page with each fixation. He has totally accepted the truism that in reading it is ideas or "mental pictures" that he is seeking, and not words. He realizes that words in themselves are quite insignificant. It is only when they are combined with other words to form ideas that they assume any air of importance whatsoever. He knows that the writer has utilized words only as a means to an end in attempting to communicate an idea or ideas to him. The very successful Accelerated Reader realizes that the author, if he were a skillful painter, could have used brushes and oils to achieve basically the same purpose.

Are you, too, starting to think this way?

Block read the next selection (Drill M) with a single fixation in the center of each block, or group of words. Hold each fixation for a normal count of 1-2-3, then move down to the center of the next block, and repeat through the selection.

Using the same procedure, go back through the selection several times until you are satisfied with your comprehension of its content.

DRILL M

The doctor was puzzled.
He again looked at the moan-

ing patient, and once again
shook his knowledgeable old

head. "Looks bad," he said.
"Temperature: 103; the pulse:

10; dark rings under the red
eyes; irregular breathing . . ."

"Another case, doctor?"
asked the worried nurse.

"Afraid so," he replied
unhappily. "Third one

admitted today!"
"Is there a cure for it,

doctor?" the nurse asked in
her most sympathetic voice.

The doctor, half choking
with emotional anxiety, an-

swered, "We can cure fall-
ing hair, broken spinal cords,

ingrown toenails, leprosy,
and tired blood, but there is

just no known cure for that
dreaded summerschoolitis!"

    You have just witnessed
a frightening scene now en-

acted again and again on our
college campuses every year.

Isn't it terrible! And to
think some people actually

have the nerve to say that
summer school *is* wonderful!

    There is a society for the
prevention of cruelty to our

dumb animal friends, or so
they say anyhow. Well, if

there is, I don't see why
they can't do something to

help the poor dumb animals
who have to go to summer

school. The least they
could do is to put all the

professors in another state
institution and not let

them out until September.
    While I am talking about

professors, let me tell you
how unreasonable and demand-

ing they are in summer. Sure,
I know they are always un-

reasonable and demanding,
but in the summer—boy!

You know they have the pure
audacity to expect you to

DRILL M

attend nearly every class!
I guess they don't realize

that students would rather
go home on Thursday than wait

until Friday to leave. And
what is even worse, they have

the nerve to expect you to be
back in time for Monday classes!

Now I ask you, what kind of a
weekend can a person have if he

doesn't get to leave until Friday, and then has to be back

Monday? There is simply no
justice left in this world.

   If you think it is awful to
have an 8:00 o'clock class, you

should have to meet at 7:30!
You don't believe me? Yes,

that's what I did say, 7:30 A.M.
No wonder the poor student's

health is injured so much by going to summer school. Anybody

knows that two hours of sleep
is not enough to maintain a

healthy body. You ask why I
only get two hours of sleep?

   Well, since you asked, I
will gladly tell you. The

reason for little sleep is
those blasted long assign-

ments. It seems that the
professors think there are

48 hours in a day. Why, some
of the teachers expect their

students to go to the library
and do (Excuse these horrible

words) *outside reading*. How
is that for crust?

But I think the worst
thing about summer school is

the last week. No kidding,
you have to work and study

60 hours a day to catch up on
all that work you didn't do

before. What? You ask why I
didn't do some of it before?

That's easy . . . well, I mean,
after all . . . you know all

work and no play . . . You know
the old saying.

Summer school is wonderful?
Well, so is bubonic plague!

Would you mind calling a
doctor? I am coming down with

a very, very bad case of that
dread disease summerschoolitis!

Drill M, which you have just completed, was printed in a column 2¼ inches wide, one inch less than the width of most softback books. If you have practiced the previous vision span drills intently, you should have increased your vision span to the point where seeing and reading 2¼ inches with one fixation in the center of the lines was entirely possible without too much difficulty.

If you did experience problems reading the 2¼ inch lines, it would tend to indicate that you need additional practice, especially with Drills A through E. If you had little if any difficulty with Drill M, then you are ready to proceed and learn the Two-Stop pattern, which, in effect, splits each page in half vertically. This "split" then requires you to read line lengths of only slightly over 1½ inches with each fixation—a width you have surely mastered by now.

Be fair with yourself. If you feel you need more practice, go back and do it now. If not, proceed.

The Two-Stop Method

In observing countless rapid readers, we have found that each one has his slightly individual way of visually covering a page, but that in most cases, the page is read with repeated "S" or "Z" movement patterns.

You will, too, in time develop your own means of covering a page in the fastest, easiest, and most effective way, but you must begin by learning the dependable and reliable Two-Stop pattern.

The exercise which follows (Drill N) will teach you the Two-Stop Method. In practicing this exercise, you are to make only two stops on each line, regardless of the number of words in either half.

As you read, try to imagine that your eyes are sponges. You are to set them in the middle of the left half-line and "soak up" all you possible can. Then you are to move your "sponges" quickly to the center of the right half-line and again "soak up" all you can. The pattern is repeated.

Repeat Drill N—paragraph by paragraph—several times on a 1-2 count. Focus left on the count of 1, and right on the count of 2. Resist any temptation to scan, or stop, more than twice on each line. If you do make more than two stops on each line, you'll see only blurs as your eyes hurry over the words, in which case, needless to say, your comprehension will not be good.

You may need to practice this entire drill many times. Make the regular Two-Stop pattern second nature to you.

DRILL N

The	alert
student	observed
as	he
read	in
Triple	*Your*
Reading	*Speed*
that the	columns of
words increased	somewhat in
width as	he went
along. They	increased, in
fact, so much	that by Drill K
they were the	same width as
the line of print	in a novel page.
It is a true fact	that some readers can
read straight down the middle	of an entire novel page
and their peripheral vision	will take in the entire line

without their eyes scanning either left or right. This is indeed quite an achievement for anyone to make in his reading improvement.

Of course,
this would be ideal.
But most of us find it
necessary to have some eye movement,
and that's surely all right provided it's
the proper left, right pattern, consciously controlled
until it becomes an automatic habit. As you read this exercise,
you note that it began with one word to the left and the next to the right.
It is quite obvious that printing a book in this manner, even a small one,
would require thousands of pages, and cost a great amount of money for the
paper and the printing, to say nothing of the extra labor to set the type.

So to
save paper
and printing costs, we
began printing two words to the
left and two words to the right. We
increased the number on each side until soon we had an
entire line printed as you find in all books which you read.
As you read this exercise, allow your vision to take in half the words
on each printed line, whether there are two or twenty. But make certain
that you make only two stops on each line—never make any more than two.

Your focal point on the left should be the center of the word or the
group of words. The same type focus is made to the right. In making the
focal change, do be certain that your eyes make only one
stop to the left and one stop to the right.
When you master this One-Line,
Two-Stop pattern,
wild horses can- not hold you back
from increased speed and improved comprehension. Notice how we alternate back and forth
with different line lengths to remind you again and again how
your eye movement pattern should be controlled. Remember that your
speed is controlled to a great extent by the deviations of fixations you
make on each line of print. Reduce the number of stops and increase speed.

If you maintain only two deviations or focuses per line,
you cannot "word-hop"—a very tiring and wasteful habit. It
works much the same way as travel time varies on a trip. If
you stop at every town along the way, your arrival time will
doubtless be much later, and you will likely be much more
fatigued than if you travel straight thru, stopping only when
it is necessary. Not only will you arrive sooner, you will probably
not be nearly so weary and tired.

Additional Practice

As soon as you totally master the Two-Stop Method on Drill N, you will want to gain additional confidence and perfect your skills further with reading and re-reading the selections which follow.

Since the number of words in each selection is given, all you will need to determine is the rate at which you are going to read each. This rate will be, to a large degree, a matter of individual progress to date. Some of you will be reading three times your beginning rate; others will have practised sufficiently to achieve rates far in excess of three times.

To illustrate how to determine the average reading time and rate, and the approximate amount of time to spend per page, we will assume that you are going to read the first selection at three times your beginning rate.

If your starting rate was 200 words per minute, you would set 600 as your rate. Then, how long will you have to read this selection which contains approximately 3,600 words?

To find out, divide 600 into 3,600. The answer is 6. This means that you must read the selection in a minimum of 6 minutes in order to maintain an average of 600 words per minute.

Next, count the pages of text in the selection to determine how much time you will have to read each page. Keep in mind that some pages will require more time to read than others. This means that you must push harder over light descriptive matter and slow up a bit when the plot thickens. You will find this is true in all that you speed read.

Since this selection is non-fiction, you'll want to follow the steps as outlined earler in "How to Preview a Chapter."

You are now ready to condition yourself to the pace and the material in the selection by reading 4 or 5 pages in the time limit you have set for each page.

Position your watch or a clock nearby so that you may observe the time. If you have a stopwatch available you will find it very useful. (You might even have a friend call time aloud for you at 5 or 10 second intervals.)

Using the Two-Stop pattern which you practiced earlier, read 4 or 5 pages (or a minute or two), being careful to spend no more nor no less than the planned time. Get the "feel" of covering the printed lines at this pace. Your comprehension may not be as good as you would like since you will be dividing your attention between reading and noting the time, but don't worry since you will soon repeat the first pages.

When you finish this exercise, question yourself to see how much you understood of the content. Now return to the first page, note the time and begin reading. You should be able to maintain your pace with less attention to the clock now.

Relax. Don't worry over a trivial point which you may not thoroughly understand as you read rapidly. This is very important. Remember that comprehension will improve rapidly with time and practice.

Go ahead and finish the entire selection. Note the time to the nearest minute when you finish. Divide the total number of reading minutes into the total number of words in the selection to determine your reading speed in words per minute.

Measure your comprehension by taking the 10 question multiple choice test and checking your answers with the key in the back of the book.

Follow the same general procedure with the other selections which follow.

The Web of Life, by John H. Storer *
(approximately 2,400 words)

Chapter 9. THE COMMUNITY THROUGH THE SEASONS

As we look at the quiet stillness of a forest we may imagine something of the feverish activity going on within it, and some of this we may see if we have the patience to watch for it.

Throughout the ages of its existence the fortunes of the great forest community are constantly fluctuating under the influence of four fundamental forces and a host of lesser ones. The long-range cycles of weather, the cycles of disease and prosperity among member groups, and the resulting changes in the influence of these groups on each other, all play a major part in the existence of a whole community. But the changing seasons of the year have the most obvious effect.

In winter the plants of the northern climates rest from their function of producing food, and all the creatures of the forest must adjust their lives to a reduced food supply. Most of the birds go south. Many animals, such as the chipmunks, woodchucks, skunks, snakes, and frogs, and many insects, retire for a long sleep during the winter. Those that remain active must depend on food stored up from the summer's harvest.

The ruffed grouse and cardinal will find it stored in the seeds, fruits, and buds of trees and bushes. The nuthatch finds the eggs of insects hidden in the bark of trees. Woodpeckers drill through the bark to find the insect larvae that winter beneath it. The red squirrel, flying squirrel, and gray squirrel live on stored seeds and nuts. Perhaps the most active and numerous animals of the forest are the white-footed mice and the shrews, and in them we see a good example of interdependence. The mice live on their stores of seeds and on what insects they can find hidden in winter retreats, while the shrews hunt day and night, digging tunnels through soil and humus and through rotting logs to capture the mice, as well as great numbers of insects.

These mammals and birds in their turn offer food to the fox, the weasel, and the barred owl, which of course can exist only in smaller numbers, since for their support they require so many of the lesser creatures.

As the snow melts and the suns of March and April warm the ground, a change comes over the forest. The low plants on the earth's surface come to life. The early insects come out of hiding and many more hatch to take advantage of the new supply of food. The skunk, the chipmunk, and several kinds of snakes, toads, and frogs wake from their winter sleep, and all include in their varied diets great numbers of insects. Now the ground grows bright with spring flowers—spring beauties, yellow adder's-tongue, hepatica, trillium, and many others. The flower buds of the elms and red maples offer food for gray squirrels. Frogs add their music to the notes of birds returning from their winter in the south. For now nature's food factory has begun again to build new life from sunlight, air, and water. The green algae in the pools, the forest plants, shrubs, and trees are all doing their share, offering their stores of energy to the creatures that come to feed on them. And the creatures respond. Insects of different kinds attack every part of every tree and plant— buds and blossoms, leaves and bark and wood. Spiders and predatory insects feed on these plant eaters, and all are in turn preyed on by the larger animals, including snakes and frogs, and by waves of migrating birds that spread up from the South to find nesting sites and hunting grounds to support their hungry young.

Many of these birds stop merely for a rest and a meal, and hurry on to find summer homes farther north. Others stay to fill every available niche in the forest and, as the leaves unfold, the branches that yesterday were bare and inhospitable, now offer shelter from weather and predators.

Dr. Arthur B. Williams of Cleveland made an interesting four-year study of the relationships of the nesting birds in a 65-acre tract of climax beech maple forest near his city. During these four years the number of pairs of nesting birds present on the tract were 136, 174, 176, and 134. This gave a yearly average of 2.3 pairs of nesting birds per acre. When one thinks of the enormous number of insects needed by a growing family of young birds, each one requiring nearly its own weight in them every day, this seems like a very small territory to supply the needs of each family. But actually the territory includes more living space than might appear, for it reaches upward to the tree tops and above, as well as along the ground. Within this territory, as we have already seen, there are many different kinds of hunting grounds. Each different kind of bird is specially adapted to hunt in its own niche, and each, having selected its own hunting territory, will defend that territory against all competitors of its own species. But many different kinds of birds may nest close together without competing, because each species occupies a different niche, while others that might compete are so scattered as to cause little trouble.

For example, Dr. Williams found four different kinds of woodpeckers nesting in the area, the pileated, hairy, downy, and red-bellied. But since each species is so specialized as to confine its hunting to a different part of the larger trees, there was apparently little competition among them. Three pairs of white-breasted nuthatches in the area might have competed with the downy woodpeckers in hunting among the bark crevices, but as their nests were widely separated, there was probably no serious competition. The chickadees and tufted titmice perhaps competed with the nuthatches, but their nests also were well scattered, so that the area allowed about 3.6 acres for each pair.

The flycatchers, living on flying insects, divided the territory, each pair of Acadian flycatchers having staked out its own separate nesting and hunting ground in a little glen by a stream. The crested flycatcher used a different part of the woods, and the wood pewees used widely separated territories in the higher areas of the forest.

On the ground and among the lower bushes, the Louisiana water thrush, wood thrush, cardinal, ovenbird, and towhee shared the territory, which totaled about two acres of hunting ground for each nesting pair. The hooded warblers and redstarts hunted chiefly at a higher level. In the leafy foliage of the taller trees the tanagers, vireos, and cerulean warblers were the chief hunters, while the blackthroated green warblers confined themselves chiefly to the upper branches of hemlocks.

Thus, every part of every tree, bush, and plant in the forest received its regular protection from its own special guardian.

As the young birds grew and left their nests, the hunting territories were less strictly guarded by their parents and finally were abandoned altogether as great numbers of young searched for their own food. In the process of growing up, many young died of accident and exposure to weather and by predator.

By summer's end, conditions began to change again for our forest community. Much of the tree and plant growth had stopped, providing less appetizing food for insects. Their own time of greatest multiplication had passed. The birds begin to move south again. The redstarts are among the first to go, followed closely by the ovenbirds. By the end of August the red-eyed vireos and wood thrushes have gone. Purple martins and chimney swifts busily hunt flying insects that seek sunshine above the dark canopy of the forest.

By the beginning of October the scarlet tanagers and hooded warblers, last of the summer birds, have gone, and now the forest is filled by great waves of southward-bound migrants coming down from the north. Hundreds of robins, thrushes of several kinds—first the hermits, then the olive-backs, veeries, and gray-cheeks stop to feed on wild grapes and on the fruits and berries of many trees and bushes. They vary this diet with beetles, grubs, and other insects, which they dig out from under dead leaves.

By early November most of the leaves have fallen and the bare tree tops again admit light to the forest floor. The robins and thrushes continue southward. Bobwhites may come in from the fields to gather beechnuts in the woods. Tracks in the early snows of late November tell of the search for food by squirrels, cottontail rabbits, red fox, white-footed mouse, and short-tailed shrew.

So the population of the forest fluctuates greatly throughout the seasons. Dr. Williams estimated the average bird population for the 65 acres that he studied to be as follows:

Permanent residents	March	May	July	Sept.	Oct.	Dec.	Jan.
woodpeckers							
barred owls							
titmice, chickadees							
cardinals, nuthatches							
towhees, etc.							
total 11 species	100	69	52	78	86	106	102

Summer residents vireos, thrushes warblers, robins flycatchers, tanagers, etc. *total 10 species*	0	365	184	195	510	2	2
Autumn and winter *visitors and transients* red-breasted nuthatches juncoes, thrushes warblers, sparrows, etc. *total 56 species*	200	505	3	295	465	218	50
Grand total	300	939	239	568	1061	326	154

All this great company of birds, mammals, and insects in Dr. Williams's study must adapt itself to the environment established and controlled by three kinds of trees—the beech, the sugar maple, and the hemlock. The tulip, red oak, red maple, and white ash play important, but secondary, roles. The chestnut once shared a dominant position until it was wiped out by blight.

With these seven trees there are 20 other lesser kinds that grow in the forest openings or borders or under the shade of the dominant trees. With them are seven species of vines, 45 common herbs and shrubs, together with 24 other rare or uncommon species; 14 ferns, 10 mosses, and six miscellaneous algae, lichen, liverwort, and sedge. Besides these, it is estimated there are between 1,200 and 1,500 different species of large fungi and other plants that live on dead organic matter from trees and plants.

Dr. Williams concluded after his study that the existence of this great forest depends on the birds, mammals, and predatory insects that protect it from its enormous population of plant-eating insects. On the other hand, the insectivorous creatures must have insects to feed them, and many of the insects, as we have seen, play an important role in preparing the forest soil and pollinating plants.

Thus, in every forest the living creatures that make up the community are actually selected by the dominant trees and the lesser plants that determine the environment in which they must live.

From all this we see that the forest is a great organization made up of many separate and indispensable parts. Some of these parts may appear to be harmful to its life. But in most cases the degree of harm or value will depend on the perfection of the control or balance that the different members achieve among themselves.

Owing to the hazards of climate and disease, this balance is never quite achieved, and its fluctuations play an important part in forest life. And on the degree of its attainment will depend the amount of life that the land can support, in other words its carrying capacity.

It is interesting to note how this principle is applied by nesting birds in the forest where, as we have just seen, each pair selects and defends enough territory to support its family. But this defense is exerted only against members of the same species, while nests of other, non-competing species might be tolerated in the same tree.

TEST

The Web of Life, Chapter 9

(Circle the letter before the most correct answer)

1. Which of the following plays the major and most obvious role in the existence of of the forest community?
   a. Long range cycles of weather.
   b. Cycles of disease and prosperity.
   c. Resulting changes of groups on each other.
   d. The changing seasons.

2. Which of the following does not occur when plants in the northern climates rest for winter?
   a. Most birds go south.
   b. Snakes retire for a long sleep.
   c. Chipmonks go south.
   d. Bears hibernate.

3. In the winter, squirrels live mainly on
   a. stored seeds and nuts.
   b. small tree buds.
   c. unharvested grain.
   d. honey stolen from bears.

4. A very vicious small animal frequently mentioned in the chapter is the
   a. field mouse.
   b. wild white rat.
   c. ring-tail skunk.
   d. shrew.

5. The fox, weasel, and horned owl exist in small numbers mainly because they
   a. are very wild and vicious.
   b. require so many lesser creatures for food.
   c. often kill each other for food.
   d. are so frequently trapped by man.

6. Different species of birds nested in the same area seem to give little competition to each other mainly because they
   a. feed at different hours.
   b. feed on different parts of plants.
   c. eat very little.
   d. soon migrate to other areas.

7. Among the first birds to migrate south in winter are the
   a. eagles.
   b. redstarts.
   c. ovenbirds.
   d. birds named in b and c.

8. The population of the forest throughout the seasons
   a. remains relatively stable.
   b. fluctuates greatly.
   c. changes twice annually.
   d. doesn't really change.

9. Creatures which feed mainly on insects are said to be
   a. insectivorous.
   b. carnivorous.
   c. herbivorous.
   d. mantises.

10. Birds of the same species seldom nest in the same tree because
    a. each parent pair selects and defends a territory to supports its family.
    b. birds of a feather never flock together.
    c. birds are by nature warlike.
    d. the young offspring would be fighting constantly.

(Check answers in back of book)

"The Cask of Amontillado," by Edgar Allan Poe
(approximately 2,600 words)

The thousand injuries of Fortunato I had borne as I best could; but when he ventured upon insult, I vowed revenge. You, who so well know the nature of my soul, will not suppose, however, that I gave utterance to a threat. *At length* I would be avenged; this was a point definitely settled—but the very definitiveness with which it was resolved, precluded the idea of risk. I must not only punish, but punish with impunity. A wrong is unredressed when retribution overtakes its redresser. It is equally unredressed when the avenger fails to make himself felt as such to him who has done the wrong.

It must be understood, that neither by word nor deed had I given Fortunato cause to doubt my good-will. I continued, as was my wont, to smile in his face, and he did not perceive that my smile *now* was at the thought of his immolation.

He had a weak point—this Fortunato—although in other regards he was a man to be respected and even feared. He prided himself on his connoisseurship in wine. Few Italians have the true virtuoso spirit. For the most part their enthusiasm is adopted to suit the time and opportunity—to practise imposture upon the British and Austrian *millionaires*. In painting and gemmary Fortunato, like his countrymen, was a quack—but in the matter of old wines he was sincere. In this respect I did not differ from him materially: I was skillful in the Italian vintages myself, and bought largely whenever I could.

It was about dusk, one evening during the supreme madness of the carnival season, that I encountered my friend. He accosted me with excessive warmth, for he had been drinking much. The man wore motley. He had on a tight-fitting parti-striped dress, and his head was surmounted by the conical cap and bells. I was so pleased to see him, that I thought I should never have done wringing his hand.

I said to him: "My dear Fortunato, you are luckily met. How remarkably well you are looking to-day! But I have received a pipe of what passes for Amontillado, and I have my doubts."

"How?" said he. "Amontillado? A pipe? Impossible! And in the middle of the carnival!"

"I have my doubts," I replied; "and I was silly enough to pay the full Amontillado price without consulting you in the matter. You were not to be found, and I was fearful of losing a bargain."

"Amontillado!"

"I have my doubts."

"Amontillado!"

"And I must satisfy them."

"Amontillado!"

"As you are engaged, I am on my way to Luchesi. If any one has a critical turn, it is he. He will tell me——"

"Luchesi cannot tell Amontillado from Sherry."

"And yet some fools will have it that his tastes is a match for your own."

"Come, let us go."

"Whither?"

"To your vaults."

"My friend, no; I will not impose upon your good nature. I perceive you have an engagement. Luchesi——"

"I have no engagement;—come."

"My friend, no. It is not the engagement, but the severe cold with which I perceive you are afflicted. The vaults are insufferably damp. They are encrusted with nitre."

"Let us go, nevertheless. The cold is merely nothing. Amontillado! You have been imposed upon. And as for Luchesi, he cannot distinguish Sherry from Amontillado."

Thus speaking, Fortunato possessed himself of my arm. Putting on a mask of black silk, and drawing a *roquelaire* closely about my person, I suffered him to hurry me to my palazzo.

There were no attendants at home; they had absconded to make merry in honor of the time. I had told them that I should not return until the morning, and had given them explicit orders not to stir from the house. These orders were sufficient, I well knew, to insure their immediate disappearance, one and all, as soon as my back was turned.

I took from their sconces two flambeaux, and giving one to Fortunato, bowed him through several suites of rooms to the archway that led into the vaults. I passed down a long and winding staircase, requesting him to be cautious as he followed. We came at length to the foot of the descent, and stood together on the damp ground of the catacombs of the Montresors.

The gait of my friend was unsteady, and the bells upon his cap jingled as he strode.

"The pipe?" said he.

"It is farther on," said I; "but observe the white webwork which gleams from these cavern walls."

He turned toward me, and looked into my eyes with two filmy orbs that distilled the rheum of intoxication.

"Nitre?" he asked, at length.

"Nitre," I replied. "How long have you had that cough?"

"Ugh! ugh! ugh!—ugh! ugh! ugh!—ugh! ugh! ugh!—ugh! ugh! ugh!—ugh! ugh! ugh!"

My poor friend found it impossible to reply for many minutes.

"It is nothing," he said at last.

"Come," I said, with decision, "we will go back; your health is precious. You are rich, respected, admired, beloved; you are happy, as once I was. You are a man to be missed. For me it is no matter. We will go back; you will be ill, and I cannot be responsible. Besides, there is Luchesi——"

Enough," he said; "the cough is a mere nothing; it will not kill me. I shall not die of a cough."

"True—true," I replied; "and, indeed, I had no intention of alarming you unnecessarily; but you should use all proper caution. A draught of this Medoc will defend us from the damps."

Here I knocked off the neck of a bottle which I drew from a long row of its fellows that lay upon the mould.

"Drink," I said, presenting him the wine.

He raised it to his lips with a leer. He paused and nodded to me familiarly, while his bells jingled.

"I drink," he said, "to the buried that repose around us."

"And I to your long life."

He again took my arm and we proceeded.

"These vaults," he said, "are extensive."

"The Montresors," I replied, "were a great and numerous family."

"I forget your arms."

"A huge human foot d'or, in a field azure; the foot crushes a serpent rampant whose fangs are imbedded in the heel."

"And the motto?"

"*Nemo me impune lacessit.*"

"Good!" he said.

The wine sparkled in his eyes and the bells jingled. My own fancy grew warm with the Medoc. We had passed through walls of piled bones, with casks and puncheons intermingling, into the inmost recesses of the catacombs. I paused again, and this time I made bold to seize Fortunato by an arm above the elbow.

"The nitre!" I said; "see, it increases. It hangs like moss upon the vaults. We are below the river's bed. The drops of moisture trickle among the bones. Come, we will go back ere it is too late. Your cough——"

"It is nothing," he said; "let us go on. But first, another draught of the Medoc."

I broke and reached him a flagon of De Grâve. He emptied it at a breath. His eyes flashed with a fierce light. He laughed and threw the bottle upward with a gesticulation I did not understand.

I looked at him in surprise. He repeated the movement—a grotesque one.

"You do not comprehend?" he said.

"Not I," I replied.

"Then you are not of the brotherhood."

"How?"

"You are not of the masons."

"Yes, yes," I said; "yes, yes."

"You? Impossible! A mason?"

"A mason," I replied.

"A sign," he said.

"It is this," I answered, producing a trowel from beneath the folds of my *roquelaire.*

"You jest," he exclaimed, recoiling a few paces. "But let us proceed to the Amontillado."

"Be it so," I said, replacing the tool beneath the cloak, and again offering him my arm. He leaned upon it heavily. We continued our route in search of the Amontillado. We passed through a range of low arches, descended, passed on, and descending again, arrived at a deep crypt, in which the foulness of the air caused our flambeaux rather to glow than flame.

At the most remote end of the crypt there appeared another less spacious. Its walls had been lined with human remains, piled to the vault overhead, in the fashion of the great catacombs of Paris. Three sides of this interior crypt were still ornamented in this manner. From the fourth the bones had been thrown down, and lay promiscuously upon the earth, forming at one point a mound of some size. Within the wall thus exposed by the displacing of the bones, we perceived a still interior recess, in depth about four feet, in width three, in height six or seven. It seemed to have been constructed for no especial use within itself, but formed merely the interval between two of the colossal supports of the roof of the catacombs, and was backed by one of their circumscribing walls of solid granite.

It was in vain that Fortunato, uplifting his dull torch, endeavored to pry into the depth of the recess. Its termination the feeble light did not enable us to see.

"Proceed," I said; "herein is the Amontillado. As for Luchesi——"

"He is an ignoramus," interrupted my friend, as he stepped unsteadily forward, while I followed immediately at his heels. In an instant he had reached the extremity of the niche, and finding his progress arrested by the rock, stood stupidly bewildered. A moment more and I had fettered him to the granite. In its surface were two iron staples, distant from each other about two feet, horizontally. From one of these depended a short chain, from the other a padlock. Throwing the links about his waist, it was but the work of a few seconds to secure it. He was too much astounded to resist. Withdrawing the key I stepped back from the recess.

"Pass your hand," I said, "over the wall; you cannot help feeling the nitre. Indeed it is *very* damp. Once more let me *implore* you to return. No? Then I must positively leave you. But I must first render you all the little attentions in my power."

"The Amontillado!" ejaculated my friend, not yet recovered from his astonishment.

"True," I replied; "the Amontillado."

As I said these words I busied myself among the pile of bones of which I have before spoken. Throwing them aside, I soon uncovered a quantity of building stone and mortar. With these materials and with the aid of my trowel, I began vigorously to wall up the entrance of the niche.

I had scarcely laid the first tier of the masonry when I discovered that the intoxication of Fortunato had in a great measure worn off. The earliest indication I had of this was a low moaning cry from the depth of the recess. It was *not* the cry of a drunken man. There was then a long and obstinate silence. I laid the second tier, and the third, and the fourth; and then I heard the furious vibrations of the chain. The noise lasted for several minutes, during which, that I might hearken to it with the more satisfaction, I ceased my labors and sat down upon the bones. When at last the clanking subsided, I resumed the trowel, and finished without interruption the fifth, the sixth, and the seventh tier. The wall was now nearly upon a level with my breast. I again paused, and holding the flambeaux over the mason-work, threw a few feeble rays upon the figure within.

A succession of loud and shrill screams, bursting suddenly from the throat of the chained form, seemed to thrust me violently back. For a brief moment I hesitated—I trembled. Unsheathing my rapier, I began to grope with it about the recess; but the thought of an instant reassured me. I placed my hand upon the solid fabric of the catacombs, and felt satisfied. I reapproached the wall. I replied to the yells of him who clamored. I re-echoed—I aided—I surpassed them in volume and in strength. I did this, and the clamorer grew still.

It was now midnight, and my task was drawing to a close. I had completed the eighth, the ninth, and the tenth tier. I had finished a portion of the last and the eleventh; there remained but a single stone to be fitted and plastered in. I struggled with its weight; I placed it partially in its destined position. But now there came from out the niche a low laugh that erected the hairs upon my head. It was succeeded by a sad voice, which I had difficulty in recognizing as that of the noble Fortunato. The voice said—

"Ha! ha! ha!—he! he!—a very good joke indeed—an excellent jest. We will have many a rich laugh about it at the palazzo—he! he! he!—over our wine—he! he! he!"

"The Amontillado!" I said.

"He! he! he!—he! he! he!—yes, the Amontillado. But is it not getting late? Will not they be awaiting us at the palazzo, the Lady Fortunato and the rest? Let us be gone."

"Yes," I said, "let us be gone."

"*For the love of God, Montresor!*"

"Yes," I said, "for the love of God!"

But to these words I hearkened in vain for a reply. I grew impatient. I called aloud:

"Fortunato!"

No answer. I called again:

"Fortunato!"

No answer still. I thrust a torch through the remaining aperture and let it fall within. There came forth in return only a jingling of the bells. My heart grew sick—on account of the dampness of the catacombs. I hastened to make an end of my labor. I forced the last stone into its position; I plastered it up. Against the new masonry I re-erected the old rampart of bones. For the half of a century no mortal has disturbed them. *In pace requiescat!*

TEST

"The Cask of Amontillado"

(Circle the letter before the most correct answer)

1. The villain desired Fortunato's death because
   a. Fortunato drank to excess.
   b. Fortunato had frequently forced injuries and insults.
   c. Fortunato was a bungling businessman.
   d. Fortunato was unclean.

2. Obviously the murder was
   a. carefully thought out and planned.
   b. totally unplanned.
   c. partially premeditated.
   d. done on the spur of the moment.

3. Fortunato's fatally weak point was that he
   a. drank too heavily.
   b. was overweight, which caused him to limp.
   c. prided himself as a connoisseur of wines.
   d. had a weak heart.

4. The fatal meeting of the two occurred during the
   a. winter season.
   b. rainy season.
   c. carnival season.
   d. summer season.

5. The ruse used to lure Fortunato to the vaults was that he was to taste for proof
   a. a cask of sherry.
   b. a pipe of amontillado.
   c. a keg of dark spirits.
   d. a foreign champagne.

6. The soon-to-be murderer pretended to be going to get which person to taste his recent purchase?
   a. Lombard.
   b. Luchesi.
   c. Montresor.
   d. Lady Fortunato.

7. When they met, Fortunato obviously
   a. was drunk.
   b. was drunk, wore motley, and was dressed in a cap with bells.
   c. was in a tight fitting parti-striped dress.
   d. was drunk and wore motley.

8. Fortunato was plagued by
   a. a severe cough.
   b. rheumatism.
   c. astigmatism.
   d. a limp.

9. The vaults contained mainly
   a. cobwebs.
   b. nitre.
   c. bones.
   d. clay.

10. The murderer sealed the tomb with how many tiers of stones?
    a. Six.
    b. Sixteen.
    c. Thirty.
    d. Eleven.

(Check answers in back of book.)

Short History of the Civil War, by Bruce Catton *
(approximately 4,300 words)

Chapter 1. A HOUSE DIVIDED

The American people in 1860 believed that they were the happiest and luckiest people in all the world, and in a way they were right. Most of them lived on farms or in very small towns, they lived better than their fathers had lived, and they knew that their children would do still better. The landscape was predominantly rural, with unending sandy roads winding leisurely across a country which was both drowsy with enjoyment of the present and vibrant with eagerness to get into the future. The average American then was in fact what he has been since only in legend, an independent small farmer, and in 1860—for the last time in American history—the products of the nation's farms were worth more than the output of its factories.

This may or may not have been the end of America's golden age, but it was at least the final, haunted moment of its age of innocence. Most Americans then, difficult as the future might appear, supposed that this or something like it would go on and on, perhaps forever. Yet infinite change was beginning, and problems left unsolved too long would presently make the change explosive, so that the old landscape would be blown to bits forever, with a bewildered people left to salvage what they could. Six hundred thousand young Americans, alive when 1860 ended, would die of this explosion in the next four years.

At bottom the coming change simply meant that the infinite ferment of the industrial revolution was about to work its way with a tremendously energetic and restless people who had a virgin continent to exploit. One difficulty was that two very different societies had developed in America, one in the North and the other in the South, which would adjust themselves to the industrial age in very different ways. Another difficulty was that the differences between these two societies were most infernally complicated by the existence in the South of the institution of chattel slavery. Without slavery, the problems between the sections could probably have been worked out by the ordinary give-and-take of politics; with slavery, they became insoluble. So in 1861 the North and the South went to war, destroying one America and beginning the building of another which is not even yet complete.

In the beginning slavery was no great problem. It had existed all across colonial America, it died out in the North simply because it did not pay, and at the turn of the century most Americans, North and South alike, considered that eventually it would go out of existence everywhere. But in 1793 Yankee Eli Whitney had invented the cotton gin—a simple device which made it possible for textile mills to use the short-staple cotton which the Southern states could grow so abundantly—and in a very short time the whole picture changed. The world just then was developing an almost limitless appetite for cotton, and in the deep South enormous quantities of cotton could be raised cheaply with slave labor. Export figures show what happened. In 1800 the United States had exported $5,000,000 worth of cotton—7 per cent of the nation's total exports. By 1810 this figure had tripled, by 1840 it had risen to $63,000,000, and by 1860 cotton exports were worth $191,000,000—57 per cent of the value of all American exports. The South had become a cotton empire, nearly four million slaves were employed, and slavery looked like an absolutely essential element in Southern prosperity.

But if slavery paid, it left men with uneasy consciences. This unease became most obvious in the North, where a man who demanded the abolition of slavery could comfort himself with the reflection that the financial loss which abolition would entail would, after all, be borne by somebody else—his neighbor to the south. In New England the fanatic William Lloyd Garrison opened a crusade, denouncing slavery as a sin and slave-owners as sinners. More effective work to organize anti-slavery sentiment was probably done by such Westerners as James G. Birney and Theodore Weld, but Garrison made the most noise—and, making it, helped to arouse most intense resentment in the South. Southerners liked being called sinners no better than anyone else. Also, they undeniably had a bear by the tail. By 1860 slave property was worth at least two billion dollars, and the abolitionists who insisted that this property be outlawed were not especially helpful in showing how this could be done without collapsing the whole Southern economy. In a natural reaction to all of this, Southerners closed ranks. It became first unhealthy and then impossible for anyone in the South to argue for the end of slavery; instead, the institution was increasingly justified as a positive good. Partly from economic pressure and partly in response to the shrill outcries of men like Garrison, the South bound itself emotionally to the institution of slavery.

Yet slavery (to repeat) was not the only source of discord. The two sections were very different, and they wanted different things from their national government.

In the North society was passing more rapidly than most men realized to an industrial base. Immigrants were arriving by the tens of thousands, there were vast areas in the West to be opened, men who were developing new industries demanded protection from cheap European imports, systems of transportation and finance were mushrooming in a fantastic manner—and, in short, this dynamic society was beginning to clamor for all sorts of aid and protection from the Federal government at Washington.

In the South, by contrast, society was much more static. There was little immigration, there were not many cities, the factory system showed few signs of growth, and this cotton empire which sold in the world market wanted as many cheap European imports as it could get. To please the South, the national government must keep its hands off as many things as possible; for many years Southerners had feared that if the North ever won control in Washington it would pass legislation ruinous to Southern interests.

John C. Calhoun of South Carolina had seen this first and most clearly. Opposing secession, he argued that any state could protect its interests by nullifying within its own borders, any act by the Federal government which it considered unconstitutional and oppressive. Always aware that the North was the faster-growing section, the South foresaw the day when the North would control the government. Then, Southerners believed, there would be legislation—a stiff high-tariff law, for instance—that would ruin the South. More and more, they developed the theory of states' rights as a matter of self-protection.

Although there were serious differences between the sections, all of them except slavery could have been settled through the democratic process. Slavery poisoned the whole situation. It was the issue that could not be compromised, the issue that made men so angry they did not want to compromise. It put a cutting edge on all arguments. It was not the only cause of the Civil War, but it was unquestionably the one cause without which the war would not have taken place. The antagonism between the sections came finally, and tragically, to express itself through the slavery issue.

Many attempts to compromise this issue had been made. All of them worked for a while; none of them lasted. Perhaps the most that can be said is that they postponed the conflict until the nation was strong enough—just barely so—to survive the shock of civil war.

There had been the Missouri Compromise, in 1820, when North and South argued whether slavery should be permitted in the land acquired by the Louisiana Purchase. Missouri was admitted as a slave state, but it was decreed that thereafter there should be no new slave states north of the parallel that marked Missouri's southern boundary. Men hoped that this would end the whole argument, although dour John Quincy Adams wrote that he considered the debate over the compromise nothing less than "a title-page to a great, tragic volume."

Then there was the Compromise of 1850, which followed the war with Mexico. Immense new territory had been acquired, and Congressman David Wilmot of Pennsylvania introduced legislation stipulating that slavery would never be permitted in any of these lands. The Wilmot Proviso failed to pass, but it was argued furiously, in Congress and out of it, for years, and immense heat was generated. In the end the aging Henry Clay engineered a new compromise. California was to be admitted as a free state, the territories of New Mexico and Utah were created without reference to the Wilmot Proviso, the slave trade in the District of Columbia was abolished, and a much stiffer act to govern the return of fugitive slaves were adopted. Neither North nor South was entirely happy with this program, but both sections accepted it in the hope that the slavery issue was now settled for good.

This hope promptly exploded. Probably nothing did more to create anti-Southern, antislavery sentiment in the North than the Fugitive Slave Act.

It had an effect precisely opposite to the intent of its backers: it aroused Northern sentiment in favor of the runaway slave, and probably caused a vast expansion in the activities of the Underground Railroad, the informal and all but unorganized system whereby Northern citizens helped Negro fugitives escape across the Canadian border. With this excitement at a high pitch, Harriet Beecher Stowe in 1852 brought out her novel *Uncle Tom's Cabin*, which sold three hundred thousand copies in its first year, won many converts to the antislavery position in the North, and, by contrast, aroused intense new resentment in the South.

On the heels of all of this, in 1854 Senator Stephen A. Douglas of Illinois introduced the fateful Kansas-Nebraska Act, which helped to put the whole controversy beyond hope of settlement.

Douglas was a Democrat, friendly to the South and well liked there. He cared little about slavery, one way or the other; what he wanted was to see the long argument settled so that the country could go about its business, which, as he saw it, included the development of the new Western country between the Missouri River and California. Specifically, Douglas wanted a transcontinental railroad, and he wanted its eastern terminus to be Chicago. Out of this desire came the Kansas-Nebraska Act.

Building the road would involve grants of public land. If the northerly route were adopted the country west of Iowa and Missouri must be surveyed and plotted, and for this a proper territorial organization of the area was needed. But the South wanted the road to go to the Pacific coast by way of Texas and New Mexico. To get Southern support for his plan, the Illinois Senator had to find powerful bait.

He found it. When he brought in a bill to create the territories of Kansas and Nebraska he put in two special provisions. One embodied the idea of "popular sovereignty"—the concept that the people of each territory would decide for themselves, when time for statehood came, whether to permit or exclude slavery—and the other specifically repealed the Missouri Compromise. The South took the bait, the bill was passed—and the country moved a long stride nearer to war.

For the Kansas-Nebraska Act raised the argument over slavery to a desperate new intensity. The moderates could no longer be heard; the stage was set for the extremists, the fire-eaters, the men who invited violence with violent words. Many Northerners, previously friendly to the South, now came to feel that the "slave power" was dangerously aggressive, trying not merely to defend slavery where it already existed but to extend it all across the national domain. Worse yet, Kansas was thrown open for settlement under conditions which practically guaranteed bloodshed.

Settlers from the North were grimly determined to make Kansas free soil; Southern settlers were equally determined to win Kansas for slavery. Missouri sent over its Border Ruffians—hardfisted drifters who crossed the line to cast illegal votes, to intimidate free-soil settlers, now and then to raid an aboli-tionist town. New England shipped in boxes of rifles, known as Beecher's Bibles in derisive reference to the Reverend Henry Ward Beecher, the Brooklyn clergyman whose antislavery fervor had led him to say that there might be spots where a gun was more useful than a Bible. The North also sent down certain free-lance fanatics, among them a lantern-jawed character named John Brown.

By 1855 all of this was causing a great deal of trouble. Proslavery patrols clashed with antislavery patrols, and there were barn-burnings, horse-stealings, and sporadic shootings. The free-soil settlement of Lawrence was sacked by a proslavery mob; in retaliation, John Brown and his followers murdered five Southern settlers near Pottawatomie Creek. When elections were held, one side or the other would complain that the polls were unfairly rigged, would put on a boycott, and then would hold an election of its own; presently there were two territorial legislatures, of clouded legality, and when the question of a constitution arose there were more boycotts, so that no one was quite sure what the voters had done.

Far from Kansas, extremists on both sides whipped up fresh tensions. Senator Charles Sumner, the humorless, self-righteous abolitionist from Massachusetts, addressed the Senate on "the crime against Kansas," loosing such unmeasured invective on the head of Senator Andrew Butler of South Carolina that Congressman Preston Brooks, also of South Carolina, a relative of Senator Butler, caned him into insensibility on the Senate floor a few days afterward. Senator William H. Seward of New York spoke vaguely but ominously of an "irrepressible conflict" that was germinating. Senator Robert Toombs of Georgia predicted a vast extension of slavery and said that he would one day auction slaves on Boston Common itself. In Alabama the eloquent William Lowndes Yancey argued hotly that the South would never find happiness except by leaving the Union and setting up an independent nation.

Now the Supreme Court added its bit. It had before it the case of Dred Scott, a Negro slave whose master, an army surgeon, had kept him for some years in Illinois and Wisconsin, where there was no slavery. Scott sued for his freedom, and in 1857 Chief Justice Roger Taney delivered the Court's opinion. That Scott's plea for freedom was denied was no particular surprise, but the grounds on which the denial was based stirred the North afresh. A Negro of slave descent, said Taney, was an inferior sort of person who could not be a citizen of any state and hence could not sue anyone; furthermore, the act by which Congress had forbidden slavery in the Northern territories was invalid because the Constitution gave slavery ironclad protection. There was no legal way in which slavery could be excluded from any territory.

An intense political ferment was working. The old Whig Party had collapsed utterly and the Democratic Party was showing signs of breaking into sectional wings. In the North there had risen the new Republican Party, an amalgamation of former Whigs, free-soilers, business leaders who wanted a central government that would protect industry, and ordinary folk who wanted a homestead act that would provide free farms in the West. The party had already polled an impressive number of votes in the Presidential campaign of 1856, and it was likely to do better in 1860. Seward of New York hoped to be its next Presidential nominee; so did Salmon P. Chase, prominent antislavery leader from Ohio; and so, also, did a lawyer and former congressman who was not nearly so well known as these two, Abraham Lincoln of Illinois.

In 1858 Lincoln ran for the Senate against Douglas. In a series of famous debates which drew national attention, the two argued the Kansas-Nebraska Act and the slavery issue up and down the state of Illinois. In the end Douglas won re-election, but he won on terms that may have cost him the Presidency two years later. Lincoln had pinned him down: Was there any lawful way in which the people of a territory could exclude slavery? (In other words, could Douglas' "popular sovereignty" be made to jibe with the Supreme Court's finding in the Dred Scott case?) Douglas replied that the thing was easy. Slavery could not live a day unless it were supported by protective local legislation. In fact, if a territorial legislature simply refused to enact such legislation, slavery would not exist regardless of what the Supreme Court had said. The answer helped Douglas win re-election, but it mortally offended the South. The threatened split in the Democratic Party came measurably nearer, and such a split could mean nothing except victory for the Republicans.

The 1850's were the tormented decade in American history. Always the tension mounted, and no one seemed able to provide an easement. The Panic of 1857 left a severe business depression, and Northern pressure for higher tariff rates and a homestead act became stronger than ever. The depression had hardly touched the South since world demand for cotton was unabated, and Southern leaders became more than ever convinced that their society and their economy were sounder and stronger than anything the North could show. There would be no tariff revision, and although Congress did pass a homestead act President James Buchanan, a Pennsylvanian but a strong friend of the South, promptly vetoed it. The administration, indeed, seemed unable to do anything. It could not even make a state out of Kansas, in which territory it was clear, by now, that a strong majority opposed slavery. The rising antagonism between the sections had almost brought paralysis to the Federal government.

And then old John Brown came out of the shadows to add the final touch.

With a mere handful of followers, Brown undertook, on the night of October 16, 1859, to seize the Federal arsenal at Harpers Ferry and with the weapons thus obtained to start a slave insurrection in the South. He managed to get possession of an enginehouse, which he held until the morning of the eighteenth; then a detachment of U.S. marines—temporarily led by Colonel Robert E. Lee of the U.S. Army—overpowered him and snuffed out his crackbrained conspiracy with bayonets and clubbed muskets. Brown was quickly tried, was convicted of treason, and early in December he was hanged. But what he had done had a most disastrous effect on men's minds. To people in the South, it seemed that Brown confirmed their worst fears: this was what the Yankee abolitionists really wanted—a servile insurrection, with unlimited bloodshed and pillage, from one end of the South to the other! The fact that some vocal persons in the North persisted in regarding Brown as a martyr simply made matters worse. After the John Brown raid the chance that the bitter sectional argument could be harmonized faded close to the vanishing point.

It was in this atmosphere that the 1860 election was held. The Republicans nominated Lincoln, partly because he was considered less of an extremist than either Seward or Chase; he was moderate on the slavery question; and agreed that the Federal government lacked power to interfere with the peculiar institution in the states. The Republican platform, however, did represent a threat to Southern interests. It embodied the political and economic program of the North—upward revision of the tariff, free farms in the West, railroad subsidies, and all the rest.

But by now a singular fatalism gripped the nation. The campaign could not be fought on the basis of these issues; men could talk only about slavery, and on that subject they could neither talk nor, for the most part, even think, with moderation. Although it faced a purely sectional opposition, the Democratic Party promptly split into halves. The Northern wing nominated Douglas, but the Southern wing flatly refused to accept the man because of his heresy in regard to slavery in the territories; it named John C. Breckinridge of Kentucky, while a fourth party, hoping desperately for compromise and conciliation, put forward John Bell of Tennessee.

The road led steadily downhill after this. The Republicans won the election, as they were bound to do under the circumstances. Lincoln got less than a majority of the popular votes, but a solid majority in the electoral college, and on March 4, 1861, he would become President of the United States . . . but not, it quickly developed, of all of the states. Fearing the worst, the legislature of South Carolina had remained in session until after the election had been held. Once it saw the returns it summoned a state convention, and this convention, in Charleston, on December 20, voted unanimously that South Carolina should secede from the Union.

This was the final catalytic agent. It was obvious that one small state could not maintain its independence; equally obvious that if South Carolina should now be forced back into the Union no one in the South ever need talk again about secession. The cotton states, accordingly, followed suit. By February, South Carolina had been joined by Mississippi, Alabama, Georgia, Florida, Louisiana, and Texas, and on February 8 delegates from the seceding states met at Montgomery, Alabama, and set up a new nation, the Confederate States of America. A provisional constitution was adopted (to be replaced in due time by a permanent document, very much like the Constitution of the United States), and Jefferson Davis of Mississippi was elected President, with Alexander Stephens of Georgia as Vice-President.

Perhaps it still was not too late for an adjustment. A new nation had come into being, but its creation might simply be a means of forcing concessions from the Northern majority; no blood had been shed, and states which voluntarily left the old Union might voluntarily return if their terms were met. Leaders in Congress worked hard, that winter of 1861, to perfect a last-minute compromise, and a committee led by Senator John J. Crittenden of Kentucky worked one out. In effect, it would re-establish the old line of the

Missouri Compromise, banning slavery in territories north of the line and protecting it south; it would let future states enter the Union on a popular sovereignty basis; it called for enforcement of the fugitive slave law, with Federal funds to compensate slaveowners whose slaves got away; and it provided that the Constitution could never be amended in such a way as to give Congress power over slavery in any of the states.

The Crittenden Compromise hung in the balance, and then collapsed when Lincoln refused to accept it. The sticking point with him was the inclusion of slavery in the territories; the rest of the program he could accept, but he wrote to a Republican associate to "entertain no proposition for a compromise in regard to the extension of slavery."

So the last chance to settle the business had gone, except for the things that might happen in the minds of two men—Abraham Lincoln and Jefferson Davis. They were strangers, very unlike each other, and yet there was an odd linkage. They were born not far apart in time or space; both came from Kentucky, near the Ohio River, and one man went south to become spokesman for the planter aristocracy, while the other went north to become representative of the best the frontier Northwest could produce. In the haunted decade that had just ended, neither man had been known as a radical. Abolitionists considered Lincoln too conservative, and Southern fire-eaters like South Carolina's Robert B. Rhett felt that Davis had been cold and unenthusiastic in regard to secession.

Now these two men faced one another, figuratively, across an ever-widening gulf, and between them they would say whether a nation already divided by mutual misunderstanding would be torn apart physically by war.

TEST

Short History of the Civil War, Chapter 1

(Circle the letter before the most correct answer)

1. Approximately how many Americans died in the Civil War?
   a. Six hundred thousand.
   b. Twelve hundred thousand.
   c. Two hundred thousand.
   d. Nineteen hundred thousand.

2. In the beginning slavery was no great problem.
   a. False.
   b. True.
   c. Yes and no.
   d. No one now knows.

3. The cotton gin was invented in 1793 by
   a. Robert Fulton.
   b. Theodore Weld.
   c. H. B. Stowe.
   d. Eli Whitney.

4. The title of the novel by Harriet Beecher Stowe which aroused anti-slavery feelings was
   a. *Brer Rabbit*.
   b. *Uncle Tom's Cabin*.
   c. *John Brown's Body*.
   d. *Snowdrift*.

5. In 1854, Senator Stephen A. Douglas of Illinois introduced the fateful
   a. Texas-New Mexico Act.
   b. Missouri Compromise.
   c. Kansas-Nebraska Act.
   d. Anti-Slavery Act.

6. One of Senator Douglas' major desires was that he wanted for America
   a. a transcontinental railroad.
   b. an end to slavery.
   c. equal taxation with representation.
   d. a lasting state of peace.

7. The idea which embodied the concept that the people of each territory would elect to permit or exclude slavery when applying for statehood was known as
   a. "political suicide."
   b. "states rights."
   c. "the big freedom."
   d. "popular sovereignty."

8. Missouri sent over hard-fisted drifters into Kansas to cast illegal votes and generally to create havoc. These groups were called
   a. Night Raiders.
   b. Vigilantes.
   c. Border Ruffians.
   d. Hard-Fisters.

9. John Brown and his followers murdered five Southern settlers near
   a. Pottawatomie Creek.
   b. Mississippi River.
   c. Ozark River.
   d. Washington Crick.

10. The Supreme Court's decision in the Dred Scott case
    a. pleased the Yankees.
    b. stirred the North afresh.
    c. caused Southern animosity.
    d. caused slavery to become unlawful.

11. In 1858, Senator Douglas won re-election over
    a. Salmon P. Chase.
    b. James Buchanan.
    c. Roger Taney.
    d. Abraham Lincoln.

12. What ten year period is called "the tormental" decade in American history?
    a. The 1850's.
    b. The 1840's.
    c. The 1870's.
    d. The 1860's.

13. John Brown's attempt to seize the arsenal at Harper's Ferry was stopped by a detachment of U. S. Marines led by
    a. General U. S. Grant.
    b. Colonel Robert E. Lee.
    c. Robert Toombs.
    d. William L. Yancey.

14. In America in 1860, the landscape, as described by Catton, was
    a. partially mechanical.
    b. predominantly rural.
    c. generally unsophisticated.
    d. mainly urban.

15. The average American of this period was in fact
    a. an independent small farmer.
    b. a factory worker.
    c. generally well-to-do.
    d. an independent small businessman.

16. Slavery died out in the North because
    a. Northerners were more religious.
    b. it simply did not pay.
    c. Southerners wanted it to.
    d. the climate was too cold for Negroes.

17. By 1860, cotton exports were worth $191,000,000. This equaled what percent of the total American exports?
    a. 13 percent.
    b. 92 percent.
    c. 57 percent.
    d. 21 percent.

18. Slaves employed in the South by 1860 totaled approximately
    a. three million.
    b. one million.
    c. ten million.
    d. four million.

19. Except for the slavery issue, the differences between North and South likely could have been settled through
    a. a later war.
    b. democratic processes.
    c. a stronger central government.
    d. serious peace talks.

20. After the Louisiana Purchase, what state from that territory was admitted as a slave state?
    a. Missouri.
    b. Texas.
    c. Louisiana.
    d. Georgia.

21. The system whereby Northern citizens helped Negro fugitives escape across the Canadian border was called the
    a. Underground Railroad.
    b. Slave Lift.
    c. Freedom Road.
    d. Underground System.

22. Members of the new Republican party in the North were mainly former members of which older party?
    a. Neutral Party.
    b. States' Rights Party.
    c. Whig Party.
    d. Democratic Party.

23. In the 1860 presidential election, Lincoln won as the result of having a
    a. majority of the popular vote.
    b. majority of the electoral votes.
    c. tie broken by congress.
    d. popular campaign in the South.

24. After Lincoln's election, the first state to secede from the Union was
    a. North Carolina.
    b. Mississippi.
    c. South Carolina.
    d. Missouri.

25. The man elected president of the new Confederate States of America was
    a. Jefferson Davis.
    b. Alexander Stephens.
    c. Robert E. Lee.
    d. John J. Crittenden.

(Check answers in back of book)

Treasure Island, by Robert Louis Stevenson
(approximately 2,400 words)

Chapter 2. BLACK DOG APPEARS AND DISAPPEARS

It was not very long after this that there occurred the first of the mysterious events that rid us at last of the captain, though not, as you will see, of his affairs. It was a bitter cold winter, with long, hard frosts and heavy gales; and it was plain from the first that my poor father was little likely to see the spring. He sank daily, and my mother and I had all the inn upon our hands, and were kept busy enough without paying much regard to our unpleasant guest.

It was one January morning, very early—a pinching, frosty morning—the cove all grey with hoar-frost, the riplapping softly on the stones, the sun still low and only touching the hilltops and shining far to seaward. The captain had risen earlier than usual, and set out down the beach, his cutlass swinging under the broad skirts of the old blue coat, his brass telescope under his arm, his hat tilted back upon his head. I remember his breath hanging like smoke in his wake as he strode off, and the last sound I heard of him, as he turned the big rock, was a loud snort of indignation, as though his mind was still running upon Dr. Livesey.

Well, mother was upstairs with father; and I was laying the breakfast-table against the captain's return, when the parlor door opened, and a man stepped in on whom I had never set my eyes before. He was a pale, tallowy creature, wanting two fingers of the left hand; and, though he wore a cutlass, he did not look much like a fighter. I had always my eye open for seafaring men, with one leg or two, and I remember this one puzzled me. He was not sailorly, and yet he had a smack of the sea about him too.

I asked him what was for his service, and he said he would take rum; but as I was going out of the room to fetch it he sat down upon a table, and motioned me to draw near. I paused where I was with my napkin in my hand.

"Come here, sonny," says he. "Come nearer here."

I took a step nearer.

"Is this here table for my mate Bill?" he asked, with a kind of leer.

I told him I did not know his mate Bill; and this was for a person who stayed in our house, whom we called the captain.

"Well," said he, "my mate Bill would be called the captain, as like as not. He has a cut on one cheek, and a mighty pleasant way with him, particularly in drink, has my mate Bill. We'll put it, for argument like, that your captain has a cut on one cheek—and we'll put it, if you like, that that cheek's the right one. Ah, well! I told you. Now, is my mate Bill in this here house?"

I told him he was out walking.

"Which way, sonny? Which way is he gone?"

And when I had pointed out the rock and told him how the captain was likely to return, and how soon, and answered a few other questions, "Ah," said he, "this'll be as good as drink to my mate Bill."

The expression of his face as he said these words was not at all pleasant, and I had my own reasons for thinking that the stranger was mistaken, even supposing he meant what he said. But it was no affair of mine, I thought; and besides, it was difficult to know what to do. The stranger kept hanging about just inside the inn door, peering round the corner like a cat waiting for a mouse. Once I stepped out myself into the road, but he immediately called me back, and as I did not obey quick enough for his fancy, a most horrible change came over his tallowy face, and he ordered me in with an oath that made me jump. As soon as I was back again he returned to his former manner, half fawning, half sneering, patted me on the shoulder, told me I was a good boy and he had taken quite a fancy to me. "I have a son of my own," said he, "as like you as two blocks, and he's all the pride of my 'art. But the great thing for boys is discipline, sonny—discipline. Now, if you had sailed along of Bill, you wouldn't have stood there to be spoke to twice—not you. That was never Bill's way, nor the way of sich as sailed with him. And here, sure enough, is my mate Bill, with a spy-glass under his arm, bless his old 'art, to be sure. You and me'll just go back into the parlour, sonny, and get behind the door, and we'll give Bill a little surprise—bless his 'art, I say again."

So saying, the stranger backed along with me into the parlour and put me behind him in the corner so that we were both hidden by the open door. I was very uneasy and alarmed, as you may fancy, and it rather added to my fears to observe that the stranger was certainly frightened himself. He cleared the hilt of his cutlass and loosened the blade in the sheath; and all the time we were waiting there he kept swallowing as if he felt what we used to call a lump in the throat.

At last in strode the captain, slammed the door behind him, without looking to the right or left, and marched straight across the room to where his breakfast awaited him.

"Bill," said the stranger in a voice that I thought he had tried to make bold and big.

The captain spun round on his heel and fronted us; all the brown had gone out of his face, and even his nose was blue; he had the look of a man who sees a ghost, or the evil one, or something worse, if anything can be; and upon my word, I felt sorry to see him all in a moment turn so old and sick.

"Come, Bill, you know me; you know an old shipmate, Bill, surely," said the stranger.

The captain made a sort of gasp.

"Black Dog!" said he.

"And who else?" returned the other, getting more at his ease. "Black Dog as ever was, come for to see his old shipmate Billy, at the Admiral Benbow inn. Ah, Bill, Bill, we have seen a sight of times, us two, since I lost them two talons," holding up his mutilated hand.

"Now, look here," said the captain; "you've run me down; here I am; well, then, speak up; what is it?"

"That's you, Bill," returned Black Dog, "you're in the right of it, Billy. I'll have a glass of rum from this dear child here, as I've took such a liking to; and we'll sit down, if you please, and talk square, like old shipmates."

When I returned with the rum, they were already seated on either side of the captain's breakfast-table—Black Dog next to the door and sitting sideways so as to have one eye on his old shipmate and one, as I thought, on his retreat.

He bade me go and leave the door wide open. "None of your keyholes for me, sonny," he said; and I left them together and retired into the bar.

For a long time, though I certainly did my best to listen, I could hear nothing but a low gabbling; but at last the voices began to grow higher, and I could pick up a word or two, mostly oaths, from the captain.

"No, no, no, no; and an end of it!" he cried once. And again, "If it comes to swinging, swing all, say I."

Then all of a sudden there was a tremendous explosion of oaths and other noises—the chair and table went over in a lump, a clash of steel followed, and then a cry of pain, and the next instant I saw Black Dog in full flight, and the captain hotly pursuing, both with drawn cutlasses, and the former streaming blood from the left shoulder. Just at the door the captain aimed at the fugitive one last tremendous cut, which would certainly have split him to the chine had it not been intercepted by our big signboard of Admiral Benbow. You may see the notch on the lower side of the frame to this day.

That blow was the last of the battle. Once out upon the road, Black Dog, in spite of his wound, showed a wonderful clean pair of heels and disappeared over the edge of the hill in half a minute. The captain, for his part, stood staring at the signboard like a bewildered man. Then he passed his hand over his eyes several times and at last turned back into the house.

"Jim," says he, "rum"; and as he spoke, he reeled a little, and caught himself with one hand against the wall.

"Are you hurt?" cried I.

"Rum," he repeated. "I must get away from here. Rum! Rum!"

I ran to fetch it, but I was quite unsteadied by all that had fallen out, and I broke one glass and fouled the tap, and while I was still getting in my own way, I heard a loud fall in the parlour, and running in, beheld the captain lying full length upon the floor. At the same instant my mother, alarmed by the cries and fighting, came running downstairs to help me. Between us we raised his head. He was breathing very loud and hard, but his eyes were closed and his face a horrible colour.

"Dear, deary me," cried my mother, "what a disgrace upon the house! And your poor father sick!"

In the meantime, we had no idea what to do to help the captain, nor any other thought but that he had got his death-hurt in the scuffle with the stranger. I got the rum, to be sure, and tried to put it down his throat, but his teeth were tightly shut and his jaws as strong as iron. It was a happy relief for us when the door opened and Doctor Livesey came in, on his visit to my father.

"Oh, doctor," we cried, "what shall we do? Where is he wounded?"

"Wounded? A fiddle-stick's end!" said the doctor. "No more wounded than you or I. The man has had a stroke, as I warned him. Now, Mrs. Hawkins, just you run upstairs to your husband and tell him, if possible, nothing about it. For my part, I must do my best to save this fellow's trebly worthless life; Jim, you get me a basin."

When I got back with the basin, the doctor had already ripped up the captain's sleeve and exposed his great sinewy arm. It was tattooed in several places. "Here's luck," "A fair wind," and "Billy Bones his fancy," were very neatly and clearly executed on the forearm; and up near the shoulder there was a sketch of a gallows and a man hanging from it—done, as I thought, with great spirit.

"Prophetic," said the doctor, touching this picture with his finger. "And now, Master Billy Bones, if that be your name, we'll have a look at the colour of your blood. Jim," he said, "are you afraid of blood?"

"No, sir," said I.

"Well, then," said he, "you hold the basin"; and with that he took his lancet and opened a vein.

A great deal of blood was taken before the captain opened his eyes and looked mistily about him. First he recognized the doctor with an unmistakable frown; then his glance fell upon me, and he looked relieved. But suddenly his colour changed, and he tried to raise himself, crying, "Where's Black Dog?"

"There is no Black Dog here," said the doctor, "except what you have on your own back. You have been drinking rum; you have had a stroke, precisely as I told you; and I have just, very much against my own will, dragged you headforemost out of the grave. Now, Mr. Bones—"

"That's not my name," he interrupted.

"Much I care," returned the doctor. "It's the name of a buccaneer of my acquaintance; and I call you by it for the sake of shortness, and what I have to say to you is this: one glass of rum won't kill you, but if you take one you'll take another and another, and I stake my wig if you don't break off short, you'll die—do you understand that?—die, and go to your own place, like the man in the Bible. Come, now, make an effort. I'll help you to your bed for once."

Between us, with much trouble, we managed to hoist him upstairs, and laid him on his bed, where his head fell back on the pillow as if he were almost fainting.

"Now, mind you," said the doctor, "I clear my conscience—the name of rum for you is death."

And with that he went off to see my father, taking me with him by the arm.

"This is nothing," he said as soon as he had closed the door. "I have drawn blood enough to keep him quiet awhile; he should lie for a week where he is—that is the best thing for him and you; but another stroke would settle him."

TEST

Treasure Island, Chapter 2

(Write T for *true*, F for *false*)

_____ 1. The time of year in the story was winter.

_____ 2. The captain's telescope was made of pure bronze.

_____ 3. There was no illness in the family at the inn.

_____ 4. The stranger who entered the door had two fingers missing on one hand.

_____ 5. The recently arrived guest ordered a cask of dark beer.

_____ 6. The stranger called the captain "my mate, William."

_____ 7. The stranger said the great thing for boys was "discipline."

_____ 8. The captain called the stranger "Black Cat."

_____ 9. They seated themselves in the captain's private bedroom.

_____10. The stranger told the boy to leave and be sure to close the door.

_____11. The boy was not at all interested in listening to the conversation.

_____12. It was soon apparent that the captain and the stranger were enemies.

_____13. The stranger was not even scratched in the ensuing fight.

_____14. The captain's cutlass was intercepted by a signboard on the inn.

_____15. The frightened captain fled rapidly from the battle scene.

_____16. The young man in the story goes by the name Jim.

_____17. The captain fell unconscious after suffering a stroke.

_____18. The doctor did not believe in "letting blood."

_____19. The doctor prescribed rum for the captain's condition.

_____20. The medical man called the captain Mr. Bones.

(Check answers in back of book)

The Time Machine, by H. G. Wells

(approximately 6,600 words)

Chapter 5

As I stood there musing over this too perfect triumph of man, the full moon, yellow and gibbous, came up out of an overflow of silver light in the north-east. The bright little figures ceased to move about below, a noiseless owl flitted by, and I shivered with the chill of the night. I determined to descend and find where I could sleep.

I looked for the building I knew. Then my eye travelled along to the figure of the White Sphinx upon the pedestal of bronze, growing distinct as the light of the rising moon grew brighter. I could see the silver birch against it. There was the tangle of rhododendron bushes, black in the pale light, and there was the little lawn. I looked at the lawn again. A queer doubt chilled my complacency. "No," said I stoutly to myself, "that was not the lawn."

But it *was* the lawn. For the white leprous face of the sphinx was towards it. Can you imagine what I felt as this conviction came home to me? But you cannot. The Time Machine was gone!

At once, like a lash across the face, came the possibility of losing my own age, of being left helpless in this strange new world. The bare thought of it was an actual physical sensation. I could feel it grip me at the throat and stop my breathing. In another moment I was in a passion of fear and running with great leaping strides down the slope. Once I fell headlong and cut my face; I lost no time in stanching the blood, but jumped up and ran on, with a warm trickle down my cheek and chin. All the time I ran I was saying to myself: "They have moved it a little, pushed it under the bushes out of the way." Nevertheless, I ran with all my might. All the time, with the certainty that sometimes comes with excessive dread. I knew that such assurance was folly, knew instinctively that the machine was removed out of my reach. My breath came with pain. I suppose I covered the whole distance from the hill crest to the little lawn, two miles perhaps, in ten minutes. And I am not a young man. I cursed aloud, as I ran, at my confident folly in leaving the machine, wasting good breath thereby. I cried aloud, and none answered. Not a creature seemed to be stirring in that moonlit world.

When I reached the lawn my worst fears were realized. Not a trace of the thing was to be seen. I felt faint and cold when I faced the empty space among the black tangle of bushes. I ran round it furiously, as if the thing might be hidden in a corner, and then stopped abruptly, with my hands clutching my hair. Above me towered the sphinx, upon the bronze pedestal, white, shining, leprous, in the light of the rising moon. It seemed to smile in mockery of my dismay.

I might have consoled myself by imagining the little people had put the mechanism in some shelter for me, had I not felt assured of their physical and intellectual inadequacy. That is what dismayed me: the sense of some hitherto unsuspected power, through whose intervention my invention had vanished. Yet, for one thing I felt assured: unless some other age had produced its exact duplicate, the machine could not have moved in time. The attachment of the levers—I will show you the method later—prevented any one from tampering with it in that way when they were removed. It had moved, and was hid, only in space. But then, where could it be?

I think I must have had a kind of frenzy. I remember running violently in and out among the moonlit bushes all round the sphinx, and startling some white animal that, in the dim light, I took for a small deer. I remember, too, late that night, beating the bushes with my clenched fist until my knuckles were gashed and bleeding from the broken twigs. Then, sobbing and raving in my anguish of mind, I went down to the great building of stone. The big hall was dark, silent, and deserted. I slipped on the uneven floor, and fell over one of the malachite tables, almost breaking my shin. I lit a match and went on past the dusty curtains, of which I have told you.

There I found a second great hall covered with cushions, upon which, perhaps, a score or so of the little people were sleeping. I have no doubt they found my second appearance strange enough, coming suddenly out of the quiet darkness and inarticulate noises and the splutter and flare of a match. For they had forgotten about matches. "Where is my Time Machine?" I began, bawling like an angry child, laying hands upon them and shaking them up together. It must have been very queer to them. Some laughed, most of them looked sorely frightened. When I saw them standing round me, it came into my head that I was doing as foolish a thing as it was possible for me to do under the circumstances, in trying to revive the sensation of fear. For, reasoning from their daylight behaviour, I thought that fear must be forgotten.

Abruptly, I dashed down the match, and, knocking one of the people over in my course, went blundering across the big dining-hall again, out under the moonlight. I heard cries of terror and their little feet running and stumbling this way and that. I do not remember all I did as the moon crept up the sky. I suppose it was the unexpected nature of my loss that maddened me. I felt hopelessly cut off from my own kind—a strange animal in an unknown world. I must have raved to and fro, screaming and crying upon God and Fate. I have a memory of horrible fatigue, as the long night of despair wore away; of looking in this impossible place and that; of groping among moon-lit ruins and touching strange creatures in the black shadows; at last, of lying on the ground near the sphinx and weeping with absolute wretchedness. I had nothing left but misery. Then I slept, and when I woke again it was full day, and a couple of sparrows were hopping round me on the turf within reach of my arm.

I sat up in the freshness of the morning, trying to remember how I had got there, and why I had such a profound sense of desertion and despair. Then things came clear in my mind. With the plain, reasonable daylight, I could look my circumstances fairly in the face. I saw the wild folly of my frenzy overnight, and I could reason with myself. "Suppose the worst?" I said. "Suppose the machine altogether lost—perhaps destroyed? It behoves me to be calm and patient, to learn the way of the people, to get a clear idea of the method of my loss, and the means of getting materials and tools; so that in the end, perhaps, I may make another." That would be my only hope, perhaps, but better than despair. And, after all, it was a beautiful and curious world.

But probably, the machine had only been taken away. Still, I must be calm and patient, find its hiding-place, and recover it by force or cunning. And with that I scrambled to my feet and looked about me, wondering where I could bathe. I felt weary, stiff, and travel-soiled. The freshness of the morning made me desire an equal freshness. I had exhausted my emotion. Indeed, as I went about my business, I found myself wondering at my intense excitement overnight. I made a careful examination of the ground about the little lawn. I wasted some time in futile questionings, conveyed, as well as I was able, to such of the little people as came by. They all failed to understand by gestures; some were simply stolid, some thought it was a jest and laughed at me. I had the hardest task in the world to keep my hands off their pretty laughing faces. It was a foolish impulse, but the devil begotten of fear and blind anger was ill curbed and still eager to take advantage of my perplexity. The turf gave better counsel. I found a groove ripped in it, about midway between the pedestal of the sphinx and the marks of my feet where, on arrival, I had struggled with the overturned machine. There were other signs of removal about, with queer narrow footprints like those I could imagine made by a sloth. This directed my closer attention to the pedestal. It was, as I think I have said, of bronze. It was not a mere block, but highly decorated with deep framed panels on either side. I went and rapped at these. The pedestal was hollow. Examining the panels with care I found them discontinuous with the frames. There were no handles or keyholes, but possibly the panels, if they were doors, as I supposed, opened from within. One thing was clear enough to my mind. It took no very great mental effort to infer that my Time Machine was inside that pedestal. But how it got there was a difficult problem.

I saw the heads of two orange-clad people coming through the bushes and under some blossom-covered apple-trees towards me. I turned smiling to them and beckoned them to me. They came, and then, pointing to the bronze pedestal, I tried to intimate my wish to open it. But at my first gesture towards this they behaved very oddly. I don't know how to convey their expression to you. Suppose you were to use a grossly improper gesture to a delicate-minded woman—it is how she would look. They went off as if they had received the last possible insult. I tried a sweet-looking little chap in white next, with exactly the same result. Somehow, this manner made me feel ashamed of myself. But, as you know, I wanted the Time Machine, and I tried him once more. As he turned off, like the others, my temper got the better of me. In three strides I was after him, had him by the loose part of his robe round the neck, and began dragging him towards the sphinx. Then I saw the horror and repugnance of his face, and all of a sudden I let him go.

But I was not beaten yet. I banged with my fist at the bronze panels, I thought I heard something stir inside—to be explicit, I thought I heard a sound like a chuckle—but I must have been mistaken. Then I got a big pebble from the river, and came and hammered till I had flattened a coil in the decorations, and the verdigris came off in powdery flakes. The delicate little people must have heard me hammering in gusty outbreaks a mile away on either hand, but nothing came of it. I saw a crowd of them upon the slopes, looking furtively at me. At last, hot and tired, I sat down to watch the place. But I was too restless to watch long; I am too Occidental for a long vigil. I could work at a problem for years, but to wait inactive for twenty-four hours—that is another matter.

I got up after a time, and began walking aimlessly through the bushes towards the hill again. "Patience," said I to myself. "If you want your machine again you must leave that sphinx alone. If they mean to take your machine away, it's little good your wrecking their bronze panels, and if they don't, you will get it back as soon as you can ask for it. To sit among all those unknown things before a puzzle like that is hopeless. That way lies monomania. Face this world. Learn its ways, watch it, be careful of too hasty guesses at its meaning. In the end you will find clues to it all." Then suddenly the humour of the situation came into my mind: the thought of the years I had spent in study and toil to get into the future age, and now my passion of anxiety to get out of it. I had made myself the most complicated and the most hopeless trap that ever a man devised. Although it was at my own expense, I could not help myself. I laughed aloud.

Going through the big palace, it seemed to me that the little people avoided me. It may have been my fancy or it may have had something to do with my hammering at the gates of bronze. Yet I felt tolerably sure of the avoidance. I was careful, however, to show no concern and to abstain from any pursuit of them, and in the course of a day or two things got back to the old footing. I made what progress I could in the language, and in addition I pushed my explorations here and there. Either I missed some subtle point, or their language was excessively simple—almost exclusively composed of concrete substantives and verbs. There seemed to be few, if any, abstract terms, or little use of figurative language. Their sentences were usually simple and of two words, and I failed to convey or understand any but the simplest propositions. I determined to put the thought of my Time Machine and the mystery of the bronze doors under the sphinx as much as possible in a corner of memory, until my growing knowledge would lead me back to them in a natural way. Yet a certain feeling, you may understand, tethered me in a circle of a few miles round the point of my arrival.

So far as I could see, all the world displayed the same exuberant richness as the Thames valley. From every hill I climbed I saw the same abundance of splendid buildings, endlessly varied in material and style, the same clustering thickets of evergreens, the same blossom-laden trees and tree-ferns. Here

and there water shone like silver, and beyond, the land rose into blue undulat-
ing hills, and so faded into the serenity of the sky. A peculiar feature, which
presently attracted my attention, was the presence of certain circular wells,
several, as it seemed to me, of a very great depth. One lay by the path up the
hill, which I had followed during my first walk. Like the others, it was
rimmed with bronze, curiously wrought, and protected by a little cupola from
the rain. Sitting by the side of these wells, and peering down into the shafted
darkness, I could see no gleam of water, nor could I start any reflection with
a lighted match. But in all of them I heard a certain sound: a thud—thud—
thud, like the beating of some big engine; and I discovered, from the flaring
of my matches, that a steady current of air set down the shafts. Further, I
threw a scrap of paper into the throat of one, and, instead of fluttering slowly
down, it was at once sucked swiftly out of sight.

After a time, too, I came to connect these wells with tall towers standing
here and there upon the slopes; for above them there was often just such a
flicker in the air as one sees on a hot day above a sun-scorched beach. Putting
things together, I reached a strong suggestion of an extensive system of subterranean ventilation, whose true import it was difficult to imagine. I was at
first inclined to associate it with the sanitary apparatus of these people. It was
an obvious conclusion, but it was absolutely wrong.

And here I must admit that I learned very little of drains and bells and
modes of conveyance, and the like conveniences, during my time in this real
future. In some of these visions of Utopias and coming times which I have
read, there is a vast amount of detail about building, and social arrangements,
and so forth. But while such details are easy enough to obtain when the whole
world is contained in one's imagination, they are altogether inaccessible to a
real traveller amid such realities as I found here. Conceive the tale of London
which a negro, fresh from Central Africa, would take back to his tribe! What
would he know of railway companies, of social movements, of telephone and
telegraph wires, of the Parcels Delivery Company, and postal orders and the
like? Yet we, at least, should be willing enough to explain these things to him!
And even of what he knew, how much could he make his untravelled friend
either apprehend or believe? Then, think how narrow the gap between a
negro and a white man of our own times, and how wide the interval between
myself and these of the Golden Age! I was sensible of much which was
unseen, and which contributed to my comfort; but save for a general impression of automatic organization, I fear I can convey very little of the difference
to your mind.

In the matter of sepulture, for instance, I could see no signs of crematoria
nor anything suggestive of tombs. But it occurred to me that possibly, there
might be cemeteries (or crematoria) somewhere beyond the range of my
explorings. This, again, was a question I deliberately put to myself, and my
curiosity was at first entirely defeated upon the point. The thing puzzled me,
and I was led to make a further remark, which puzzled me still more: that
aged and infirm among this people there were none.

I must confess that my satisfaction with my first theories of an automatic civilization and a decadent humanity did not long endure. Yet I could think of no other. Let me put my difficulties. The several big palaces I had explored were mere living places, great dining-halls and sleeping apartments. I could find no machinery, no appliances of any kind. Yet these people were clothed in pleasant fabrics that must at times need renewal, and their sandals, though undecorated, were fairly complex specimens of metalwork. Somehow such things must be made. And the little people displayed no vestige of a creative tendency. There were no shops, no workshops, no sign of importations among them. They spent all their time in playing gently, in bathing in the river, in making love in a half-playful fashion, in eating fruit and sleeping. I could not see how things were kept going.

Then, again, about the Time Machine: something, I knew not what, had taken it into the hollow pedestal of the White Sphinx. *Why?* For the life of me I could not imagine. Those waterless wells, too, those flickering pillars. I felt I lacked a clue. I felt—how shall I put it? Suppose you found an inscription, with sentences here and there in excellent plain English, and interpolated therewith, others made up of words, of letters even, absolutely unknown to you? Well, on the third day of my visit, that was how the world of Eight Hundred and Two Thousand Seven Hundred and One presented itself to me!

That day, too, I made a friend—of a sort. It happened that, as I was watching some of the little people bathing in a shallow, one of them was seized with cramp and began drifting downstream. The main current ran rather swiftly, but not too strongly for even a moderate swimmer. It will give you an idea, therefore, of the strange deficiency in these creatures, when I tell you that none made the slightest attempt to rescue the weakly crying little thing which was drowning before their eyes. When I realized this, I hurriedly slipped off my clothes, and, wading in at a point lower down, I caught the poor mite and drew her safe to land. A little rubbing of limbs soon brought her round, and I had the satisfaction of seeing she was all right before I left her. I had got to such a low estimate of her kind that I did not expect any gratitude from her. In that, however, I was wrong.

This happened in the morning. In the afternoon I met my little woman, as I believe it was, as I was returning towards my centre from an exploration, and she received me with cries of delight and presented me with a big garland of flowers—evidently made for me and me alone. The thing took my imagination. Very possibly I had been feeling desolate. At any rate I did my best to display my appreciation of the gift. We were soon seated together in a little stone arbour, engaged in conversation, chiefly of smiles. The creature's friendliness affected me exactly as a child's might have done. We passed each other flowers, and she kissed my hands. I did the same to hers. Then I tried talk, and found that her name was Weena, which though I don't know what it meant, somehow seemed appropriate enough. That was the beginning of a queer friendship which lasted a week, and ended—as I will tell you!

She was exactly like a child. She wanted to be with me always. She tried to follow me everywhere, and on my next journey out and about it went to my heart to tire her down and leave her at last, exhausted and calling after me rather plaintively. But the problems of the world had to be mastered. I had not, I said to myself, come into the future to carry on a miniature flirtation. Yet her distress when I left her was very great, her expostulations at the parting were sometimes frantic, and I think, altogether, I had as much trouble as comfort from her devotion. Nevertheless she was, somehow, a very great comfort. I thought it was mere childish affection that made her cling to me. Until it was too late, I did not clearly know what I had inflicted upon her when I left her. Nor until it was too late did I clearly understand what she was to me. For, by merely seeming fond of me, and showing in her weak, futile way that she cared for me, the little doll of a creature presently gave my return to the neighbourhood of the White Sphinx almost the feeling of coming home; and I would watch for her tiny figure of white and gold so soon as I came over the hill.

It was from her, too, that I learned that fear had not yet left the world. She was fearless enough in the daylight, and she had the oddest confidence in me; for once, in a foolish moment, I made threatening grimaces at her, and she simply laughed at them. But she dreaded the dark, dreaded shadows, dreaded black things. Darkness to her was the one thing dreadful. It was a singularly passionate emotion, and it set me thinking and observing. I discovered then, among other things, that these little people gathered into the great houses after dark, and slept in droves. To enter upon them without a light was to put them into a tumult of apprehension. I never found one out of doors, or one sleeping alone within doors, after dark. Yet I was still such a blockhead that I missed the lesson of that fear, and in spite of Weena's distress I insisted upon sleeping away from these slumbering multitudes.

It troubled her greatly, but in the end her odd affection for me triumphed, and for five of the nights of our acquantance, including the last night of all, she slept with her head pillowed on my arm. But my story slips away from me as I speak of her. It must have been the night before her rescue that I was awakened about dawn. I had been restless, dreaming most disagreeably that I was drowned, and that sea-anemones were feeling over my face with their soft palps. I woke with a start, and with an odd fancy that some greyish animal had just rushed out of the chamber. I tried to get to sleep again, but I felt restless and uncomfortable. It was that dim grey hour when things are just creeping out of darkness, when everything is colourless and clear cut, and yet unreal. I got up, and went down into the great hall, and so out upon the flagstones in front of the palace. I thought I would make a virtue of necessity, and see the sunrise.

The moon was setting, and the dying moonlight and the first pallor of dawn were mingled in a ghastly half-light. The bushes were inky black, the ground a sombre grey, the sky colourless and cheerless. And up the hill I thought I could see ghosts. There several times, as I scanned the slope, I saw white figures. Twice I fancied I saw a solitary white, ape-like creature running rather quickly up the hill, and once near the ruins I saw a leash of them carrying some dark body. They moved hastily. I did not see what became of them.

It seemed that they vanished among the bushes. The dawn was still indistinct, you must understand. I was feeling that chill, uncertain, early-morning feeling you may have known. I doubted my eyes.

As the eastern sky grew brighter, and the light of the day came on and its vivid colouring returned upon the world once more, I scanned the view keenly. But I saw no vestige of my white figures. They were mere creatures of the half-light. "They must have been ghosts," I said; "I wonder whence they dated." For a queer notion of Grant Allen's came into my head, and amused me. If each generation die and leave ghosts, he argued, the world at last will get overcrowded with them. On that theory they would have grown innumerable some Eight Hundred Thousand Years hence, and it was no great wonder to see four at once. But the jest was unsatisfying, and I was thinking of these figures all the morning, until Weena's rescue drove them out of my head. I associated them in some indefinite way with the white animal I had startled in my first passionate search for the Time Machine. But Weena was a pleasant substitute. Yet all the same, they were soon destined to take far deadlier possession of my mind.

I think I have said how much hotter than our own was the weather of this Golden Age. I cannot account for it. It may be the sun was hotter, or the earth nearer the sun. It is usual to assume that the sun will go on cooling steadily in the future. But people, unfamiliar with such speculations as those of the younger Darwin, forget that the planets must ultimately fall back one by one into the parent body. As these catastrophes occur, the sun will blaze with renewed energy; and it may be that some inner planet had suffered this fate. Whatever the reason, the fact remains that the sun was very much hotter than we know it.

Well, one very hot morning—my fourth, I think—as I was seeking shelter from the heat and glare in a colossal ruin near the great house where I slept and fed, there happened this strange thing: clambering among these heaps of masonry, I found a narrow gallery, whose end and side windows were blocked by fallen masses of stone. By contrast with the brilliancy outside, it seemed at first impenetrably dark to me. I entered it groping, for the change from light to blackness made spots of colour swim before me. Suddenly I halted spellbound. A pair of eyes, luminous by reflection against the daylight without, was watching me out of the darkness.

The old instinctive dread of wild beasts came upon me. I clenched my hands and steadfastly looked into the glaring eyeballs. I was afraid to turn. Then the thought of the absolute security in which humanity appeared to be living came to my mind. And then I remembered that strange terror of the dark. Overcoming my fear to some extent, I advanced a step and spoke. I will admit that my voice was harsh and ill-controlled. I put out my hand and touched something soft. At once the eyes darted sideways, and something white ran past me. I turned with my heart in my mouth, and saw a queer little ape-like figure, its head held down in a peculiar manner, running across the sunlit space behind me. It blundered against a block of granite, staggered aside, and in a moment was hidden in a black shadow beneath another pile of ruined masonry.

My impression of it is, of course, imperfect; but I know it was a dull white, and had strange large greyish-red eyes; also that there was flaxen hair on its head and down its back. But, as I say, it went too fast for me to see distinctly. I cannot even say whether it ran on all-fours, or only with its forearms held very low. After an instant's pause I followed it into the second heap of ruins. I could not find it at first; but, after a time in the profound obscurity, I came upon one of those round well-like openings of which I have told you, half closed by a fallen pillar. A sudden thought came to me. Could this Thing have vanished down the shaft? I lit a match, and, looking down, I saw a small, white, moving creature, with large bright eyes which regarded me steadfastly as it retreated. It made me shudder. It was so like a human spider! It was clambering down the wall, and now I saw for the first time a number of metal foot and hand rests forming a kind of ladder down the shaft. Then the light burned my fingers and fell out of my hand, going out as it dropped, and when I had lit another the little monster had disappeared.

I do not know how long I sat peering down that well. It was not for some time that I could succeed in persuading myself that the thing I had seen was human. But, gradually, the truth dawned on me: that Man had not remained one species, but had differentiated into two distinct animals: that my graceful children of the Upper-world were not the sole descendants of our generation, but that this bleached, obscene, nocturnal Thing, which had flashed before me, was also heir to all the ages.

I thought of the flickering pillars and of my theory of an underground ventilation. I began to suspect their true import. And what, I wondered, was this Lemur doing in my scheme of a perfectly balanced organization? How was it related to the indolent serenity of the beautiful Upper-worlders? And what was hidden down there, at the foot of that shaft? I sat upon the edge of the well telling myself that, at any rate, there was nothing to fear, and that there I must descend for the solution of my difficulties. And withal I was absolutely afraid to go! As I hesitated, two of the beautiful Upper-world people came running in their amorous sport across the daylight in the shadow. The male pursued the female, flinging flowers at her as he ran.

They seemed distressed to find me, my arm against the overturned pillar, peering down the well. Apparently it was considered bad form to remark these apertures; for when I pointed to this one, and tried to frame a question about it in their tongue, they were still more visibly distressed and turned away. But they were interested by my matches, and I struck some to amuse them. I tried them again about the well, and again I failed. So presently I left them, meaning to go back to Weena, and see what I could get from her. But my mind was already in revolution; my guesses and impressions were slipping and sliding to a new adjustment. I had now a clue to the import of these wells, to the ventilating towers, to the mystery of the ghosts; to say nothing of a hint at the meaning of the bronze gates and the fate of the

Time Machine! And very vaguely there came a suggestion towards the solution of the economic problem that had puzzled me.

Here was the new view. Plainly, this second species of Man was subterranean. There were three circumstances in particular which made me think that its rare emergence above ground was the outcome of a long-continued underground look common in most animals that live largely in the dark—the white fish of the Kentucky caves, for instance. Then, those large eyes, with that capacity for reflecting light, are common features of nocturnal things—witness the owl and the cat. And last of all, that evident confusion in the sunshine, that hasty yet fumbling awkward flight towards dark shadow, and that peculiar carriage of the head while in the light—all reinforced the theory of an extreme sensitiveness of the retina.

Beneath my feet, then, the earth must be tunnelled enormously, and these tunnellings were the habitat of the new race. The presence of ventilating shafts and wells along the hill slopes—everywhere, in fact, except along the river valley—showed how universal were its ramifications. What so natural, then, as to assume that it was in this artificial Under-world that such work as was necessary to the comfort of the daylight race was done? The notion was so plausible that I at once accepted it, and went on to assume the how of this splitting of the human species. I dare say you will anticipate the shape of my theory; though, for myself, I very soon felt that it fell far short of the truth.

At first, proceeding from the problems of our own age, it seemed clear as daylight to me that the gradual widening of the present merely temporary and social difference between the Capitalist and the Labourer, was the key to the whole position. No doubt it will seem grotesque enough to you—and wildly incredible!—and yet even now there are existing circumstances to point that way. There is a tendency to utilize underground space for the less ornamental purposes of civilization; there is the Metropolitan Railway in London, for instance, there are new electric railways, there are subways, there are underground workrooms and restaurants, and they increase and multiply. Evidently, I thought, this tendency had increased till Industry had gradually lost its birthright in the sky. I mean that it had gone deeper and deeper into larger and ever larger underground factories, spending a still-increasing amount of its time therein, till, in the end—! Even now, does not an East-end worker live in such artifical conditions as practically to be cut off from the natural surface of the earth?

Again, the exclusive tendency of richer people—due, no doubt, to the increasing refinement of their education, and the widening gulf between them and the rude violence of the poor—is already leading to the closing, in their interest, of considerable portions of the surface of the land. About London, for instance, perhaps half the prettier country is shut in against intrusion. And this same widening gulf—which is due to the length and expense of the higher educational process and the increased facilities for and temptations towards refined habits on the part of the rich—will make that exchange between class and class, that promotion by intermarriage which at present retards the splitting of our species along lines of social stratification, less and less frequent. So, in the end, above ground you must have the Haves, pursuing pleasure and comfort and beauty, and below ground the Have-nots, the Workers getting continually adapted to the conditions of their labour. Once they were there, they would no doubt have to pay rent, and not a little of it, for the ventilation of their caverns; and if they refused, they would starve or be suffocated for arrears. Such of them as were so constituted as to be miserable and rebellious would die; and, in the end, the balance being permanent, the survivors would become as well adapted to the conditions of underground life, and as happy in their way, as the Upper-world people were to theirs. As it seemed to me, the refined beauty and the etiolated pallor followed naturally enough.

The great triumph of Humanity I had dreamed of took a different shape in my mind. It had been no such triumph of moral education and general co-operation as I had imagined. Instead, I saw a real aristocracy, armed with a perfected science and working to a logical conclusion the industrial system of to-day. Its triumph had not been simply a triumph over Nature, but a triumph over Nature and the fellow-man. This, I must warn you, was my theory at the time. I had no convenient cicerone in the pattern of the Utopian books. My explanation may be absolutely wrong. I still think it is the most plausible one. But even on this supposition the balanced civilization that was at last attained must have long since passed its zenith, and was now far fallen into decay. The too-perfect security of the Upper-worlders had led them to a slow movement of degeneration, to a general dwindling in size, strength, and intelligence. That I could see clearly enough already. What had happened to the Under-grounders I did not yet suspect; but from what I had seen of the Morlocks—that, by the by, was the name by which these creatures were called —I could imagine that the modification of the human type was even far more profound than among the "Eloi," the beautiful race that I already knew.

Then came troublesome doubts. Why had the Morlocks taken my Time Machine? For I felt sure it was they who had taken it. Why, too, if the Eloi were masters, could they not restore the machine to me? And why were they so terribly afraid of the dark? I proceeded, as I have said, to question Weena about this Under-world, but here again I was disappointed. At first she would not understand my questions, and presently she refused to answer them. She shivered as though the topic was unendurable. And when I pressed her, perhaps a little harshly, she burst into tears. They were the only tears, except my own, I ever saw in that Golden Age. When I saw them I ceased abruptly to trouble about the Morlocks, and was only concerned in banishing these signs of the human inheritance from Weena's eyes. And very soon she was smiling and clapping her hands, while I solemnly burned a match.

TEST

Time Machine, Chapter 5

(Write T for *true*, F for *false*)

—— 1. In the first paragraph, the moon is described as full and rising.

—— 2. The wisteria bushes appeared black in the pale light.

—— 3. He discovered that the Time Machine was gone.

—— 4. The Time Traveler experienced no noticeable fear.

—— 5. The Time Traveler states that he was not a young man.

—— 6. The sphinx rested upon a bronze pedestal.

—— 7. His search for his machine soon proved fruitful.

—— 8. When he went to the great building of stone, he found some of the little people sleeping.

—— 9. He made no inquiry about his vehicle there.

—10. After a fitful sleep he awoke to find himself surrounded by many strange creatures.

—11. He immediately set about to build another Time Machine.

—12. He discovered the pedestal under the sphinx to be hollow.

—13. The little people were very helpful in supplying complete information about the sphinx and the pedestal.

—14. He banged upon the walls of the pedestal with a big pebble.

—15. In a few days the Time Traveler completely mastered the strange but simple language of the little people.

—16. He compares the surrounding area of the strange world with the Thames valley.

—17. He soon noted certain square wells.

—18. The wells seemed to suck in air.

—19. The writer speaks of this future time as the Golden Age.

—20. He observed many cemeteries scattered about the countryside.

—21. The little people were apparently not much interested in work.

—22. The year in time was 802,701 A.D.

—23. The Time Traveler rescued a small dog from the river.

—24. His young friend's name was Weena.

—25. He describes Weena as being "exactly like a child."

—26. Weena feared daylight, but had no concern for darkness.

—27. Weena insisted that they not sleep near the others.

—28. The Time Traveler describes the weather as uncomfortably cold.

——29. In a darkened narrow gallery he was confronted by a pair of glowing eyes.

——30. What he saw appeared to be a queer little ape-like figure.

——31. He soon decided that the creature was a second species of Man.

——32. The Time Traveler resolved that this second species was subterranean by nature.

——33. These underground beings were called Morlocks.

(Check answers in back of book)

Dr. Jekyll and Mr. Hyde, by Robert Louis Stevenson
(approximately 7,000 words)

HENRY JEKYLL'S FULL STATEMENT OF THE CASE

I was born in the year 18—— to a large fortune, endowed besides with excellent parts, inclined by nature to industry, fond of the respect of the wise and good among my fellowmen, and thus, as might have been supposed, with every guarantee of an honourable and distinguished future. And indeed the worst of my faults was a certain impatient gaiety of disposition, such as has made the happiness of many, but such as I found it hard to reconcile with my imperious desire to carry my head high, and wear a more than commonly grave countenance before the public. Hence it came about that I concealed my pleasures; and that when I reached years of reflection, and began to look round me and take stock of my progress and position in the world, I stood already committed to a profound duplicity of life. Many a man would have even blazoned such irregularities as I was guilty of; but from the high views that I had set before me, I regarded and hid them with an almost morbid sense of shame. It was thus rather the exacting nature of my aspirations that any particular degradation in my faults, that made me what I was, and, with even a deeper trench than in the majority of men, severed in me those provinces of good and ill which divide and compound man's dual nature. In this case, I was driven to reflect deeply and inveterately on that hard law of life, which lies at the root of religion and is one of the most plentiful springs of distress. Though so profound a double-dealer, I was in no sense a hypocrite; both sides of me were in dead earnest; I was no more myself when I laid aside restraint and plunged in shame, than when I laboured, in the eye of day, at the furtherance of knowledge or the relief of sorrow and suffering. And it chanced that the direction of my scientific studies, which led wholly towards the mystic and the transcendental, reacted and shed a strong light on this consciousness of the perennial war among my members. With every day, and from both sides of my intelligence, the moral and the intellectual, I thus drew steadily nearer to that truth, by whose partial discovery I have been doomed to such a dreadful shipwreck: that man is not truly one, but truly two. I say two, because the state of my own knowledge does not pass beyond that point. Others will follow, others will outstrip me on the same lines; and I hazard the guess that man will be ultimately known for a mere polity of multifarious, incongruous, and independent denizens. I for my part, from the nature of my life, advanced infallibly in one direction and in one direction only. It was on the moral side, and in my own person, that I learned to recognise the thorough and primitive duality of man; I saw that, of the two natures that contended in the field of my consciousness, even if I could rightly be said to be either, it was only because I was radically both; and from an early date, even before the course of my scientific discoveries had begun to suggest the most naked possibility of such a miracle, I had learned to dwell with pleasure, as a beloved day-dream, on the thought of the separation of these elements. If each, I told myself, could but be housed in separate identities, life would be relieved of all that was unbearable; the unjust might go his way, delivered from the aspirations and remorse of his more upright twin; and the just could walk steadfastly and securely on his upward path, doing the good things in which he found his pleasure, and no longer exposed to disgrace and penitence by the hands of this extraneous evil. It was the curse of mankind that these incongruous faggots were thus bound together—that in the agonised womb of consciousness, these polar twins should be continuously struggling. How, then, were they dissociated?

I was so far in my reflections when, as I have said, a side light began to shine upon the subject from the laboratory table. I began to perceive more deeply than it has ever yet been stated, the trembling immateriality, the mist-like transience, of this seemingly so solid body in which we walk attired. Certain agents I found to have the power to shake and to pluck back that fleshly vestment, even as a wind might toss the curtains of a pavilion. For two good reasons, I will not enter deeply into this scientific branch of my confession. First, because I have been made to learn that the doom and burthen of our life is bound for ever on man's shoulders, and when the attempt is made to cast it off, it but returns upon us with more unfamiliar and more awful pressure. Second, because, as my narrative will make, alas! too evident, my discoveries were incomplete. Enough, then, that I not only recognised my natural body for the mere aura and effulgence of certain of the powers that made up my spirit, but managed to compound a drug by which these powers should be dethroned from their supremacy, and a second form and countenance substituted, none the less natural to me because they were the expression, and bore the stamp, of lower elements in my soul.

I hesitated long before I put this theory to the test of practice. I knew well that I risked death; for any drug that so potently controlled and shook the very fortress of identity, might by the least scruple of an overdose or at the least inopportunity in the moment of exhibition, utterly blot out that im-material tabernacle which I looked to it to change. But the temptation of a discovery so singular and profound, at last overcame the suggestions of alarm. I had long since prepared my tincture; I purchased at once, from a firm of wholesale chemists, a large quantity of a particular salt which I knew, from my experiments, to be the last ingredient required; and late one accursed night, I compounded the elements, watched them boil and smoke together in the glass, and when the ebullition had subsided, with a strong glow of courage, drank off the potion.

The most racking pangs succeeded: a grinding in the bones, deadly nausea, and a horror of the spirit that cannot be exceeded at the hour of birth or death. Then these agonies began swiftly to subside, and I came to myself as if out of a great sickness. There was something strange in my sensations, something indescribably new and, from its very novelty, incredibly sweet. I felt younger, lighter, happier in body; within I was conscious of a heady reck- lessness, a current of disordered sensual images running like a mill race in my fancy, a solution of the bonds of obligation, an unknown but not an innocent freedom of the soul. I knew myself, at the first breath of this new life, to be more wicked, tenfold more wicked, sold a slave to my original evil; and the thought, in that moment, braced and delighted me like wine. I stretched out my hands, exulting in the freshness of these sensations; and in the act, I was suddenly aware that I had lost in stature.

There was no mirror, at that date, in my room; that which stands beside me as I write, was brought there later on for the very purpose of these transformations. The night, however, was far gone into the morning—the morning, black as it was, was nearly ripe for the conception of the day— the inmates of my house were locked in the most rigorous hours of slumber; and I determined, flushed as I was with hope and triumph, to venture in my new shape as far as to my bedroom. I crossed the yard, wherein the constella- tions looked down upon me, I could have thought, with wonder, the first creature of that sort that their unsleeping vigilance had yet disclosed to them; I stole through the corridors, a stranger in my own house; and coming to my room, I saw for the first time the appearance of Edward Hyde.

I must speak by theory alone, saying not that which I know, but that which I suppose to be most probable. The evil side of my nature, to which I had now transferred the stamping efficacy, was less robust and less developed than the good which I had just deposed. Again, in the course of my life, which had been, after all, nine-tenths a life of effort, virtue, and control, it had been much less exercised and much less exhausted. And hence, as I think, it came about that Edward Hyde was so much smaller, slighter, and younger than Henry Jekyll. Even as good shone upon the countenance of the one, evil was written broadly and plainly on the face of the other. Evil besides (which I must still believe to be the lethal side of man) had left on that body an imprint of deformity and decay. And yet when I looked upon that ugly idol in the glass, I was conscious of no repugnance, rather of a leap of welcome. This, too, was myself. It seemed natural and human. In my eyes it bore a livelier image of the spirit, it seemed more express and single, than the imperfect and divided countenance I had been hitherto accustomed to call mine. And in so far I was doubtless right. I have observed that when I wore the semblance of Edward Hyde, none could come near to me at first without a visible misgiving of the flesh. This, as I take it, was because all human beings, as we meet them, are commingled out of good and evil: and Edward Hyde, alone in the ranks of mankind, was pure evil.

I lingered but a moment at the mirror: the second and conclusive experi- ment had yet to be attempted; it yet remained to be seen if I had lost my identity beyond redemption and must flee before daylight from a house that was no longer mine; and hurrying back to my cabinet, I once more prepared and drank the cup, once more suffered the pangs of dissolution, and came to myself once more with the character, the stature, and the face of Henry Jekyll.

That night I had come to the fatal cross roads. Had I approached my discovery in a more noble spirit, had I risked the experiment while under the empire of generous or pious aspirations, all must have been otherwise, and from these agonies of death and birth, I had come forth an angel instead of a fiend. The drug had no discrimnating action; it was neither diabolical nor divine; it but shook the doors of the prison house of my disposition; and like the captives of Philippi, that which stood within ran forth. At that time my virtue slumbered; my evil, kept awake by ambition, was alert and swift to seize the occasion; and the thing that was projected was Edward Hyde. Hence, although I had now two characters as well as two appearances, one was wholly evil, and the other was still the old Henry Jekyll, that incongruous compound of whose reformation and improvement I had already learned to despair. The movement was thus wholly towards the worse.

Even at that time, I had not yet conquered my aversion to the dryness of a life of study. I would still be merrily disposed at times; and as my pleasures were (to say the least) undignified, and I was not only well known and highly considered, but growing towards the elderly man, this incoherency of my life was daily growing more unwelcome. It was on this side that my new power tempted me until I fell in slavery. I had but to drink the cup, to doff at once the body of the noted professor, and to assume, like a thick cloak, that of Edward Hyde. I smiled at the notion; it seemed to me at the time to be humourous; and I made my preparations with the most studious care. I took and furnished the house in Soho, to which Hyde was tracked by the police; and engaged as housekeeper a creature whom I well knew to be silent and unscrupulous. On the other side, I announced to my servants that a Mr. Hyde (whom I described) was to have full liberty and power about my house in the square; and to parry mishaps, I even called and made myself a familiar object, in my second character. I next drew up that will to which you so much objected; so that if anything befell me in the person of Dr. Jekyll, I could enter on that of Edward Hyde without pecuniary loss. And thus fortified, as I supposed, on every side, I began to profit by the strange immunities of my position.

Men have before hired bravos to transact their crimes, while their own person and reputation sat under shelter. I was the first that ever did so for his pleasures. I was the first that could thus plod in the public eye with a load of genial respectability, and in a moment, like a schoolboy, strip off these lendings and spring headlong into the sea of liberty. But for me, in my impenetrable mantle, the safety was complete. Think of it—I did not even exist! Let me but escape into my laboratory door, give me but a second or two to mix and swallow the draught that I had always standing ready; and whatever he had done, Edward Hyde would pass away like the stain of breath upon a mirror; and there in his stead, quietly at home, trimming the midnight lamp in his study, a man who could afford to laugh at suspicion, would be Henry Jekyll.

The pleasures which I made haste to seek in my disguise were, as I have said, undignified; I would scarce use a harder term. But in the hands of Edward Hyde, they soon began to turn towards the monstrous. When I would come back from these excursions, I was often plunged into a kind of wonder at my vicarious depravity. This familiar that I called out of my own soul, and sent forth alone to do his good pleasure, was a being inherently malign and villainous; his every act and thought centered on self; drinking pleasure with bestial avidity from any degree of torture to another; relentless like a man of stone. Henry Jekyll stood at times aghast before the acts of Edward Hyde; but the situation was apart from ordinary laws, and insidiously relaxed the grasp of conscience. It was Hyde, after all, and Hyde alone, that was guilty. Jekyll was no worse; he woke again to his good qualities seemingly unimpaired; he would even make haste, where it was possible, to undo the evil done by Hyde. And thus his conscience slumbered.

Into the details of the infamy at which I thus connived (for even now I can scarce grant that I committed it) I have no design of entering; I mean but to point out the warnings and the successive steps with which my chastisement approached. I met with one accident which, as it brought on no consequence, I shall no more than mention. An act of cruelty to a child aroused against me the anger of a passer-by, whom I recognised the other day in the person of your kinsman; the doctor and the child's family joined him; there were moments when I feared for my life; and at last, in order to pacify their too just resentment, Edward Hyde had to bring them to the door, and pay them in a cheque drawn in the name of Henry Jekyll. But this danger was easily eliminated from the future, by opening an account at another bank in the name of Edward Hyde himself; and when, by sloping my own hand backward, I had supplied my double with a signature, I thought I sat beyond the reach of fate.

Some two months before the murder of Sir Danvers, I had been out for one of my adventures, had returned at a late hour, and woke the next day in bed with somewhat odd sensations. It was in vain I looked about me; in vain I saw the decent furniture and tall proportions of my room in the square; in vain that I recognised the pattern of the bed curtains and the design of the mahogany frame; something still kept insisting that I was not where I was, that I had not wakened where I seemed to be, but in the little room in Soho where I was accustomed to sleep in the body of Edward Hyde. I smiled to myself, and, in my psychological way began lazily to inquire into the elements of this illusion, occasionally, even as I did so, dropping back into a comfortable morning doze. I was still so engaged when, in one of my more wakeful moments, my eyes fell upon my hand. Now the hand of Henry Jekyll (as you have often remarked) was professional in shape and size: it was large, firm, white, and comely. But the hand which I now saw, clearly enough, in the yellow light of a mid-London morning, lying half shut on the bed clothes, was lean, corded, knuckly, of a dusky pallor, and thickly shaded with a swart growth of hair. It was the hand of Edward Hyde.

I must have stared upon it for near half a minute, sunk as I was in the mere stupidity of wonder, before terror woke up in my breast as sudden and startling as the crash of cymbals; and bounding from my bed, I rushed to the mirror. At the sight that met my eyes, my blood was changed into something exquisitely thin and icy. Yes, I had gone to bed Henry Jekyll, I had awakened Edward Hyde. How was this to be explained? I asked myself; and then, with another bound of terror—how was it to be remedied? It was well on in the morning; the servants were up; all my drugs were in the cabinet—a long journey down two pair of stairs, through the back passage, across the open court and through the anatomical theatre, from where I was then standing horror-struck. It might indeed be possible to cover my face; but of what use was that, when I was unable to conceal the alteration in my stature? And then with an overpowering sweetness of relief, it came back upon my mind that the servants were already used to the coming and going of my second self. I had soon dressed, as well as I was able, in clothes of my own size; had soon passed through the house, where Bradshaw stared and drew back at seeing Mr. Hyde at such an hour and in such a strange array; and ten minutes later, Dr. Jekyll had returned to his own shape and was sitting down, with a darkened brow, to make a feint of breakfasting.

Small indeed was my appetite. This inexplicable incident, this reversal of my previous experience, seemed, like the Babylonian finger on the wall, to be spelling out the letters of my judgment; and I began to reflect more seriously than ever before on the issues and possibilities of my double existence. That part of me which I had the power of projecting, had lately been much exercised and nourished; it had seemed to me of late as though the body of Edward Hyde had grown in stature, as though (when I wore that form) I were conscious of a more generous tide of blood; and I began to spy a danger that, if this were much prolonged, the balance of my nature might be permanently overthrown, the power of voluntary change be forfeited, and the character of Edward Hyde become irrevocably mine. The power of the drug had not been always equally displayed. Once, very early in my career, it had totally failed me; since then I had been obliged on more than one occasion to double, and once, with infinite risk of death, to treble the amount; and these rare uncertainties had cast hitherto the sole shadow on my contentment. Now, however, and in the light of that morning's accident, I was led to remark that whereas, in the beginning, the difficulty had been to throw off the body of Jekyll, it had of late gradually but decidedly transferred itself to the other side. All things therefore seemed to point to this: that I was slowly losing hold of my original and better self, and becoming slowly incorporated with my second and worse.

Between these two, I now felt I had to choose. My two natures had memory in common, but all other faculties were most unequally shared between them. Jekyll (who was composite) now with the most sensitive apprehensions, now with a greedy gusto, projected and shared in the pleasures and adventures of Hyde; but Hyde was indifferent to Jekyll, or but remembered him as the mountain bandit remembers the cavern in which he conceals himself from pursuit. Jekyll had more than a father's interest; Hyde had more than a son's indifference. To cast in my lot with Jekyll, was to die to those appetites which I had long secretly indulged and had of late begun to pamper. To cast it in with Hyde, was to die to a thousand interests and aspirations, and to become, at a blow and for ever, despised and friendless. The bargain might appear unequal; but there was still another consideration in the scales; for while Jekyll would suffer smartingly in the fires of abstinence, Hyde would be not even conscious of all that he had lost. Strange as my circumstances were, the terms of this debate are as old and commonplace as man; much the same inducements and alarms cast the die for any tempted and trembling sinner; and it fell out with me, as it falls with so vast a majority of my fellows, that I chose the better part and was found wanting in the strength to keep to it.

Yes, I preferred the elderly and discontented doctor, surrounded by friends and cherishing honest hopes; and bade a resolute farewell to the liberty, the comparative youth, the light step, leaping impulses and secret pleasures, that I had enjoyed in the disguise of Hyde. I made this choice perhaps with some unconscious reservation, for I neither gave up the house in Soho, nor destroyed the clothes of Edward Hyde, which still lay ready in my cabinet. For two months, however, I was true to my determination; for two months I led a life of such severity as I had never before attained to, and enjoyed the compensations of an approving conscience. But time began at last to obliterate the freshness of my alarm; the praises of conscience began to grow into a thing of course; I began to be tortured with throes and longings, as of Hyde struggling after freedom; and at last, in an hour of moral weakness, I once again compounded and swallowed the transforming draught.

I do not suppose that, when a drunkard reasons with himself upon his vice, he is once out of five hundred times affected by the dangers that he runs through his brutish, physical insensibility; neither had I, long as I had considered my position, made enough allowance for the complete moral insensibility and insensate readiness to evil, which were the leading characters of Edward Hyde. Yet it was by these that I was punished. My devil had been long caged, he came out roaring. I was conscious, even when I took the draught, of a more unbridled, a more furious propensity to ill. It must have been this, I suppose, that stirred in my soul that tempest of impatience with which I listened to the civilities of my unhappy victim; I declare, at least, before God, no man morally sane could have been guilty of that crime upon so pitiful a provocation; and that I struck in no more reasonable spirit than that in which a sick child may break a plaything. But I had voluntarily stripped myself of all those balancing instincts by which even the worst of us continues to walk with some degree of steadiness among temptations; and in my case, to be tempted, however slightly, was to fall.

Instantly the spirit of hell awoke in me and raged. With a transport of glee, I mauled the unresisting body, tasting delight from every blow; and it was not till weariness had begun to succeed, that I was suddenly, in the top fit of my delirium, struck through the heart by a cold thrill of terror. A mist dispersed; I saw my life to be forfeit; and fled from the scene of these excesses, at once glorifying and trembling, my lust of evil gratified and stimulated, my love of life screwed to the topmost peg. I ran to the house in Soho, and (to make assurance doubly sure) destroyed my papers; thence I set out through the lamplit streets, in the same divided ecstasy of mind, gloating on my crime, light-headedly devising others in the future, and yet still hastening and still hearkening in my wake for the steps of the avenger. Hyde had a song upon his lips as he compounded the draught, and as he drank it, pledged the dead man. The pangs of transformation had not done tearing him, before Henry Jekyll, with streaming tears of gratitude and remorse, had fallen upon his knees and lifted his clasped hands to God. The veil of self-indulgence was rent from head to foot. I saw my life as a whole: I followed it up from the days of childhood, when I had walked with my father's hand, and through the self-denying toils of my professional life, to arrive again and again, with the same sense of unreality, at the damned horrors of the evening. I could have screamed aloud; I sought with tears and prayers to smother down the crowd of hideous images and sounds with which my memory swarmed against me; and still, between the petitions, the ugly face of my iniquity stared into my soul. As the acuteness of this remorse began to die away, it was succeeded by a sense of joy. The problem of my conduct was solved. Hyde was thenceforth impossible; whether I would or not, I was now confined to the better part of my existence; and O, how I rejoiced to think it! with what willing humility, I embraced anew the restrictions of natural life! with what sincere renunciation, I locked the door by which I had so often gone and come, and ground the key under my heel!

The next day came the news that the murder had been overlooked, that the guilt of Hyde was patent to the world, and that the victim was a man high in public estimation. It was not only a crime, it had been a tragic folly. I think I was glad to know it; I think I was glad to have my better impulses thus buttressed and guarded by the terrors of the scaffold. Jekyll was now my city of refuge; let but Hyde peep out an instant, and the hands of all men would be raised to take and slay him.

I resolved in my future conduct to redeem the past; and I can say with honesty that my resolve was fruitful of some good. You know yourself how earnestly in the last months of last year, I laboured to relieve suffering; you know that much was done for others, and that the days passed quietly, almost happily for myself. Nor can I truly say that I wearied of this beneficent and innocent life; I think instead that I daily enjoyed it more completely; but I was still cursed with my duality of purpose; and as the first edge of my penitence wore off, the lower side of me, so long indulged, so recently chained down, began to growl for license. Not that I dreamed of resuscitating Hyde; the bare idea of that would startle me to frenzy: no, it was in my own person, that I was once more tempted to trifle with my conscience; and it was as an ordinary secret sinner, that I at last fell before the assaults of temptation.

There comes an end to all things; the most capacious measure is filled at last; and this brief condescension to my evil finally destroyed the balance of my soul. And yet I was not alarmed; the fall seemed natural, like a return to the old days before I had made my discovery. It was a fine, clear, January day, wet underfoot where the frost had melted, but cloudless overhead; and the Regent's Park was full of winter chirrupings and sweet with spring odours. I sat in the sun on a bench; the animal within me licking the chops of memory; the spiritual side a little drowsed, promising subsequent penitence, but not yet moved to begin. After all, I reflected, I was like my neighbours; and then I smiled, comparing myself with other men, comparing my active good-will with the lazy cruelty of their neglect. And at the very moment of that vainglorious thought, a qualm came over me, a horrid nausea and the most deadly shuddering. These passed away, and left me faint; and then as in its turn the faintness subsided, I began to be aware of a change in the temper of my thoughts, a greater boldness, a contempt of danger, a solution of the bonds of obligation. I looked down; my clothes hung formlessly on my shrunken limbs; the hand that lay on my knee was corded and hairy. I was once more Edward Hyde. A moment before I had been safe of all men's respect, wealthy, beloved—the cloth laying for me in the dining room at home; and now I was the common quarry of mankind, hunted, houseless, a known murderer, thrall to the gallows.

My reason wavered, but it did not fail me utterly. I have more than once observed that, in my second character, my faculties seemed sharpened to a point and my spirits more tensely elastic; thus it came about that, where Jekyll perhaps might have succumbed, Hyde rose to the importance of the moment. My drugs were in one of the presses of my cabinet; how was I to reach them? That was the problem that (crushing my temples in my hands) I set myself to solve. The laboratory door I had closed. If I sought to enter by the house, my own servants would consign me to the gallows. I saw I must employ another hand, and thought of Lanyon. How was he to be reached? how persuaded? Supposing that I escaped capture in the streets, how was I to make my way into his presence and how should I, an unknown and displeasing visitor, prevail on the famous physician to rifle the study of his colleague, Dr. Jekyll? Then I remembered that of my original character, one part remained to me: I could write my own hand; and once I had conceived that kindling spark, the way that I must follow became lighted up from end to end.

Thereupon I arranged my clothes as best I could, and summoning a passing hansom, drove to an hotel in Portland Street, the name of which I chanced to remember. At my appearance (which was indeed comical enough, however tragic, a fate these garments covered) the driver could not conceal his mirth. I gnashed my teeth upon him with a gust of devilish fury; and the smile withered from his face—happily for him—yet more happily for myself, for in another instant I had certainly dragged him from his perch. At the inn, as I entered, I looked about me with so black a countenance as made the attendants tremble; not a look did they exchange in my presence; but obsequiously took my orders, led me to a private room, and brought me wherewithal to write. Hyde in danger of his life was a creature new to me; shaken with inordinate anger, strung to the pitch of murder, lusting to inflict pain. Yet the creature was astute; mastered his fury with a great effort of the will;

composed his two important letters, one to Lanyon and one to Poole; and that he might receive actual evidence of their being posted, sent them out with directions that they should be registered.

Thenceforward, he sat all day over the fire in the private room, gnawing his nails; there he dined, sitting alone with his fears, the waiter visibly quailing before his eye; and thence, when the night was fully come, he set forth in the corner of a closed cab, and was driven to and fro about the streets of the city. He, I say—I cannot say, I. That child of Hell had nothing human; nothing lived in him but fear and hatred. And when at last, thinking the driver had begun to grow suspicious, he discharged the cab and ventured on foot, attired in his misfitting clothes, an object marked out for observation, into the midst of the nocturnal passengers, these two base passions raged within him like a temptest. He walked fast, hunted by his fears, chattering to himself, skulking through the less frequented thoroughfares, counting the minutes that still divided him from midnight. Once a woman spoke to him, offering, I think, a box of lights. He smote her in the face, and she fled.

When I came to myself at Lanyon's, the horror of my old friend perhaps affected me somewhat: I do not know; it was at least but a drop in the sea to the abhorrence with which I looked back upon these hours. A change had come over me. It was no longer the fear of the gallows, it was the horror of being Hyde that racked me. I received Lanyon's condemnation partly in a dream; it was partly in a dream that I came home to my own house and got into bed. I slept after the prostration of the day, with a stringent and profound slumber which not even the nightmares that wrung me could avail to break. I awoke in the morning shaken, weakened, but refreshed. I still hated and feared the thought of the brute that slept within me, and I had not of course forgotten the appalling dangers of the day before; but I was once more at home, in my own house and close to my drugs, and gratitude for my escape shone so strong in my soul that it almost rivalled the brightness of hope.

I was stepping leisurely across the court after breakfast, drinking the chill of the air with pleasure, when I was seized again with those indescribable sensations that heralded the change; and I had but the time to gain the shelter of my cabinet, before I was once again raging and freezing with the passions of Hyde. It took on this occasion a double dose to recall me to myself; and alas! six hours after, as I sat looking sadly in the fire, the pangs returned, and the drug had to be readministered. In short, from that day forth it seemed only by a great effort as of gymnastics, and only under the immediate stimulation of the drug, that I was able to wear the countenance of Jekyll. At all hours of the day and night, I would be taken with the premonitory shudder; above all, if I slept, or even dozed for a moment in my chair, it was always as Hyde that I awakened. Under the strain of this continually impending doom and by the sleeplessness to which I now condemned myself, ay, even beyond what I had thought possible to man, I became, in my own person, a creature eaten up and emptied by fever, languidly weak both in body and mind, and solely occupied by one thought: the horror of my other self. But when I slept, or when the virtue of the medicine wore off, I would leap almost without transition (for the pangs of transformation grew daily less marked) into the possession of a fancy brimming with images of terror, a soul boiling with causeless hatreds, and a body that seemed not strong enough to contain the raging energies of life. The powers of Hyde seemed to have grown with the sickliness of Jekyll. And certainly the hate that now divided them was equal on each side. With Jekyll, it was a thing of vital instinct. He had now seen the full deformity of that creature that shared with him some of the phenomena of consciousness, and was co-heir with him to death: and beyond these links of community, which in themselves made the most poignant part of his distress, he thought of Hyde, for all his energy of life, as of something not only hellish but inorganic. This was the shocking thing; that the slime of the pit seemed to utter cries and voices; that the amorphous dust gesticulated and sinned; that what was dead, and had no shape, should usurp the offices of life. And this again, that that insurgent horror was knit to him closer than a wife, closer than an eye; lay caged in his flesh, where he heard it mutter and felt it struggle to be born; and at every hour of weakness, and in the confidence of slumber, prevailed against him, and deposed him out of life. The hatred of Hyde for Jekyll, was of a different order. His terror of the gallows drove him continually to commit temporary suicide, and return to his subordinate station of a part instead of a person; but he loathed the necessity, he loathed the despondency into which Jekyll was now fallen, and he resented the dislike with which he was himself regarded. Hence the apelike tricks that he would play me, scrawling in my own hand blasphemies on the pages of my books, burning the letters and destroying the portrait of my father; and indeed, had it not been for his fear of death, he would long ago have ruined himself in order to involve me in the ruin. But his love of life is wonderful; I go further: I, who sicken and freeze at the mere thought of him, when I recall the abjection and passion of this attachment, and when I know how he fears my power to cut him off by suicide, I find it in my heart to pity him.

It is useless, and the time awfully fails me, to prolong this description; no one has ever suffered such torments, let that suffice; and yet even to these, habit brought—no, not alleviation—but a certain callousness of soul, a certain acquiescence of despair; and my punishment might have gone on for years, but for the last calamity which has now fallen, and which has finally severed me from my own face and nature. My provision of the salt, which had never been renewed since the date of the first experiment, began to run low. I sent out for a fresh supply, and mixed the draught; the ebullition followed, and the first change of colour, not the second; I drank it and it was without efficiency. You will learn from Poole how I have had London ransacked: it was in vain; and I am now persuaded that my first supply was impure, and that it was that unknown impurity which lent efficacy to the draught.

About a week has passed, and I am now finishing this statement under the influence of the last of the old powders. This, then, is the last time, short of a miracle, that Henry Jekyll can think his own thoughts or see his own face (now how sadly altered!) in the glass. Nor must I delay too long to bring my writing to an end; for if my narrative has hitherto escaped destruction, it has been by a combination of great prudence and great good luck. Should the throes of change take me in the act of writing it, Hyde will tear it in pieces; but if some time shall have elapsed after I have laid it by, his wonderful selfishness and circumscription to the moment will probably save it once again from the action of his apelike spite. And indeed the doom that is closing on us both, has already changed and crushed him. Half an hour from now, when I shall again and for ever reindue that hated personality, I know how I shall sit shuddering and weeping in my chair, or continue, with the most strained and fearstruck ecstasy of listening, to pace up and down this room (my last earthly refuge) and give ear to every sound of menace. Will Hyde die upon the scaffold? or will he find courage to release himself at the last moment? God knows; I am careless; this is my true hour of death, and what is to follow concerns another than myself. Here then, as I lay down the pen and proceed to seal up my confession, I bring the life of that unhappy Henry Jekyll to an end.

TEST

Dr. Jekyll and Mr. Hyde: "Henry Jekyll's Full Statement of the Case"

(Circle the letter before the most correct answer)

1. Henry Jekyll was born in the
   a. 1600's.
   b. 1700's.
   c. 1900's.
   d. 1800's.

2. Dr. Jekyll states that he was born
   a. to no fortune.
   b. to a large fortune.
   c. to a modest fortune.
   d. in dire poverty.

3. At an early age in his life he was quite aware of a distinct
   a. duplicity.
   b. hunger for wealth.
   c. need for love.
   d. lack of affection.

4. The direction of Jekyll's scientific studies led toward
   a. the mystical.
   b. the orthodox.
   c. the transcendental.
   d. both a and c.

5. He developed the means to separate the good and the evil in himself through
   a. an electrical device.
   b. a compounded drug.
   c. an electronic device.
   d. self-hypnosis.

6. He hesitated to experiment with the above because he feared
   a. criticism.
   b. God.
   c. death.
   d. himself.

7. The last ingredient or device needed for his experiment was
   a. a particular salt.
   b. a transformer.
   c. a vial of elixir.
   d. a voltmeter.

8. He describes his first sensations after starting the experiment as
   a. racking pangs.
   b. grinding in the bones.
   c. a deadly nausea.
   d. all of the above.

9. The first visually noticeable change he observed in himself was
   a. a loss in stature.
   b. a loss in weight.
   c. an increase in height.
   d. long hair on his face.

10. He was able to view his changed form by sneaking to
    a. the lake.
    b. his lab.
    c. his wife's room.
    d. his bedroom.

11. His reflection was then that of
    a. Edgar Hyde.
    b. Edward Hyde.
    c. Elbert Hyde.
    d. Egbert Hyde.

12. Mr. Hyde is described as being
    a. an image of the devil.
    b. smaller, slighter, and younger than Jekyll.
    c. the image of a monster.
    d. larger, heavier, and older than Jekyll.

13. The ugly idol's reflection brought upon Jekyll
    a. no repugnance.
    b. only terror.
    c. a bitter hatred.
    d. total awe.

14. For Hyde, Dr. Jekyll took and furnished a house in
    a. London.
    b. Winchester.
    c. Hyde Park.
    d. Soho.

15. Mr. Hyde's pleasures, at first, are described by Jekyll as being
    a. monstrous.
    b. undignified.
    c. heinous.
    d. depraved.

16. The murder mentioned is that of
    a. Sir Edwards.
    b. Prince Prospero.
    c. Sir David Davis.
    d. Sir Danvers.

17. When Dr. Jekyll noticed that his hand had not made its accustomed change from that of Mr. Hyde, he was
    a. in bed at his home.
    b. in bed at the rented place.
    c. in his office.
    d. out on the public street.

18. The servant who was startled by Mr. Hyde, still in Jekyll's clothes, was named
    a. Bradshaw.
    b. Wellingham.
    c. McHenry.
    d. Bradley.

19. Soon Dr. Jekyll's greatest fear was that
    a. Hyde would dominate.
    b. Jekyll would dominate.
    c. he was being dishonest.
    d. the police would catch him.

20. The writer describes his Jekyll self as
    a. saint-like.
    b. totally evil.
    c. totally good.
    d. a composite.

21. Jekyll was able to resist transforming himself into Hyde for
    a. two years.
    b. two months.
    c. two days.
    d. two weeks.

22. Finally, the unwanted change to Hyde overtook Jekyll
    a. in the park.   c. in his home.
    b. on a bench.   d. in the park on a bench.

23. He hurriedly departed the place mentioned above
    a. on a horse.   c. in a hansom.
    b. in a motorcar.   d. on foot.

24. The two letters posted from the hotel were addressed to
    a. Lanyon and Poole.   c. Hyde and Poole.
    b. Jekyll and Portland.   d. Lanyon and Jekyll.

25. Soon he was able to wear the countenance of Jekyll only
    a. with Lanyon's aid.   c. at night.
    b. with drugs.   d. during the day.

(Check answers in back of book)

DEVELOP YOUR SKILLS FURTHER

To determine your approximate words per minute rate on materials you read outside this book, it is necessary that you have some quick and relatively accurate means of ascertaining the number of words to be read.

HOW TO ESTIMATE BOOK WORDAGE

It is relatively easy to find the approximate word length of a book by employing this method:

1. First, determine the average number of words on a typical full page. You may do this by either one of the two means explained below.
    A. Actually count all the words on a full page. Count all words and every word as one no matter the number of letters in it.
    B. A quicker means is to count the words on four full lines and then divide the total by 4 to get the average number of words per line. In softback books, the average usually runs between 10 and 15. Next, count the number of lines (whether full lines or not) and multiply the number of lines (usually between 26 and 35) by the average number of words per line. This will give you a fairly close estimate of the number of words on each page.
2. Second, find out how many pages there are in the text of the book. Be careful to note on what page the text actually begins. Sometimes it starts on the page numbered 1, but often it starts on page 5, 7, 9, or 15, or later. Then deduct from the total number of pages of text any numbered pages that are solely graphics—maps, photographic inserts, etc.
3. Third, multiply the total number of pages of text by the average number of words per page.
4. Fourth, round this figure off to the lower thousand. For instance, if you come up with 53,826, just call it an even 53,000 words. This adjusts the

figure for more accuracy by allowing for late starts on title pages, and early finishes at the ends of chapters.

HOW TO ESTIMATE COLUMN WORDAGE

It is very simple to estimate the number of words in newspaper and magazine articles if you have a ruler handy.

Measure off a vertical inch of print. Count the words it contains. Then, to get a close estimate of the number of words in any columnar article, just measure to see how many inches it is. Multiply the number of inches by the average number of words to an inch and you'll have your figure.

SETTING YOUR PACE

Now that you know the number of words you are going to read, it will be necessary to determine the rate at which you are going to read. This will be, to a large degree, a matter of individual progress to date. Some of you will be reading only three times your beginning rate, others will have achieved greater speed.

To review how to set a pace, we will assume that you are going to read at a rate three times faster than your beginning average. If your beginning rate was 200 words per minute, you would set 600 as your rate. How long will you have to read a book of say 36,000 words?

To find out, divide the rate into the total number of words in the book. In this case, 600 would be divided into 36,000. The answer is 60. This means that the book must be read in 60 minutes in order to maintain an average of 600 words per minute. Apply this formula to the particular book you are about to Acceleread.

Now that you know the total amount of time for reading the whole text, it is necessary to divide the assignment into four equal parts so that you may more evenly allocate attention to the entire reading for more complete comprehension. Therefore, we are going to "quarter and mark" our book. This means that we will divide the book (the actual text, excluding introductory front matter) into four equal parts.

Tear a sheet of paper into four strips which will serve as bookmarks. At the top of each strip write the number of minutes that are allowed for each quarter. In our example we have 60 minutes for reading. We would mark the first strip with the number 15, the second with 30, the third with 45, and the fourth with 60. The strips are then inserted bookmark fashion at the pages that are one-quarter, one-half, three-quarters through the text, and the final one at the last page of text. These strips may be inserted "stairstep fashion" so that the first is lowest and the others are graduated so that when the book is closed the numbers may be read on all four strips without opening the book. This will enable you to tell at a glance how you are doing as you read the book.

Next, in order to determine the pace you should maintain throughout the book, determine how many pages are in each quarter. Suppose there are 30 pages. Going along with our example mentioned earlier, this means that there are approximately 30 seconds to cover each page, based upon the 15 minutes allowed for each quarter. With your particular book you may have more or less time, depending on the number of words, pages, and the rate you will read.

Assuming that you have already previewed the book thoroughly, you are now ready to condition yourself by reading a few pages in the time you have set per page.

Using the Two-Stop pattern you have practiced earlier, read several pages (perhaps the first chapter) being careful to spend the amount of time planned per page. Get the "feel" of covering the printed lines at this pace. Your comprehension may not be as thorough as you would like since you will be dividing your attention between the reading and checking the time, but don't worry since you will repeat the first pages soon.

When you finish this practice in the first chapter, question yourself to see what understanding of the content you received. Return to the first page and again begin reading, noting time less frequently. You may be sure that you are maintaining a satisfactory pace if you remove the first marker at approximately the time lapse as indicated on it. Remember that you are now reading rapidly enough that you will have plenty of time to check back if necessary to fill in some little detail that you may have missed. This checking back will be less and less necessary as you gain, through practice, confidence in your new reading methods.

Finish the entire book if possible at one "sitting;" it will help your comprehension. Note the time to the nearest minute when you finish. Now divide the total number of reading minutes into the total number of words in the book to determine your speed in words per minute.

Repeat this process with more and more books. You will find that with practice both speed and comprehension will improve dramatically. But again we must emphasize that you must continue to discipline yourself at all times.

Appendix 1

Techniques of Better Study

Do you know how to regulate and control your study time? Do you know how to squeeze the last drop of advantage from that time you spend "hitting the old books?" This section contains some valuable hints about the "how and why" of studying. Learn the hints and use them; you'll be pleasantly surprised with your upgraded study efficiency.

A DEFINITE TIME

Set aside a specific time in your daily schedule which shall be known and observed as your "Official Study Period." Also set a minimum and a realistic maximum amount of time to be spent in study. Observe these limits.

You can never truthfully say, "The teacher didn't make a specific assignment for next class, so there is nothing to study." If there is no "assignment" for the following class meeting, use your study time for a good review. Then you won't have to "cram" for your next big test.

You can't afford to allow non-study activities to take any part of your study period. Tell your friends not to call or come by for a visit during your study hours. Don't answer the telephone; leave instructions that you are "out."

How much time will you need? You'll be able to determine this shortly after your courses begin. Of course, the total time you will need will be determined by the number and type of courses, and your own study efficiency. However, the college catalogs mention the fact that one semester's credit hour should require two hours of preparation weekly. This means that a three-hour course should get six hours of outside study each week.

A DEFINITE PLACE

Where should you study? Any place—a desk in your room, a kitchen table—where you can be reasonably comfortable and away from the mainstream of activity in your home, office, or dormitory. Get away from the television set, little brother, and friends.

It is important that the spot you select be one which you normally do not use except for study. If it's the table where you play cards, it's very easy to think about the last game there rather than about what you're trying to study.

STUDY PROPS

You use specific items for a bath—soap, towels, etc. As a matter of fact, if you don't use the right things, your bath won't be much of a success. The same is true for study.

Use a desk or table of adequate size and height. And this is *most* important . . . clear it of *everything* except the actual book or materials you require to properly study that one particular subject you are working on. You can't concentrate very well on writing a theme for English class if you have in front of you a math book with 20 problems awaiting you, and half a dozen other tasks and assignments. Work and worry only about what you have before you at the moment. The other subjects can be taken care of easier after you complete one assignment more satisfactorily because you are giving it your full attention.

Sit in a straight chair, not one that's too comfortable—unless you plan to snooze.

LIGHT AND TEMPERATURE

Concentrate good light on your desk. The rest of the room should be lighted very softly. With a soft light in the background, distant objects— paintings, wallpaper, statues, etc.—won't have as much chance of stealing your interest and attention.

The temperature should be a degree or so cooler than "normal." You likely will become sleepy if the room is too warm. Arrange for some fresh air circulation if at all possible.

DURATION OF STUDY

How long can you study effectively at one sitting? It depends on several factors, but it is relatively safe to say that 30 to 45 minutes is about the maximum you can study without taking a break, whether scheduled or not. So, it is wise to schedule a five-minute break about every half to three-quarter hour.

When you do break, get completely away from your work, both physically and mentally. Take a walk through or around the house. Get a drink of water or a glass of milk. Reward yourself.

After five minutes, you'll return to your study mentally and physically refreshed. This study-break habit can enable you to study for longer periods of time with the minimum amount of fatigue and maximum efficiency. Try it and see.

Appendix 2

Higher Test Scores

To make high scores on tests and examinations, you must: 1) know your subject well; and 2) know how to take tests.

Suggestions to help you know your subject well have been discussed at length in various other portions of this book. We shall be concerned here with the techniques of taking tests more efficiently.

Test scores are very important even though they may not accurately measure what you really know—they measure only what you put on paper. But it is a fact that very often, in school and industry, you either succeed or fail because of what you put on paper.

Too often low scores on examinations are caused by lack of skill in test-taking rather than any real lack of study or lack of knowledge of the subject.

What can you do to get those scores up and keep them up?

PREPARE MENTALLY AND PSYCHOLOGICALLY

First, make certain that you have done everything reasonably possible to know your subject. Keep up with assignments and homework preceding the test. Review thoroughly, study notes, test yourself. This sort of thorough preparation will help instill confidence—an important prerequisite for making better scores.

Secondly, after you've thoroughly prepared, after you've done all you reasonably can do before the test, don't worry. What's the very worst thing that could happen? You could fail the test. Of course you don't want to fail it, but ask yourself, if I do fail this one test, will it really make much difference a hundred years from now? Now, will it? Don't worry. Worry is a non-profit institution. Develop a little faith and confidence in yourself.

TESTS ARE ROUTINE

When the test is given to you, remember that it is really no different from a daily assignment. The only real difference is that you will have to budget your time more carefully.

Quickly preview the test. Note the number and type of questions, and the grade point value of each. Make quick decisions about the amount of time you will allow yourself for each part of the test. You will find that pencilled marginal notations of the time to be allowed will aid you greatly in getting through the test during the period.

Next, place your watch where you can see it easily, or note the time on the classroom clock. This is important, since you will essentially be working against the clock. The time will be your constant reminder of how well you are succeeding.

Then, dive right in. Answer the first question. Concentrate all of your attention on it; forget all other questions at the moment. When you have completed it, skip some space, and tackle question 2. Don't hesitate, don't sit around and worry; take *action*. Action keeps fear away.

Proceed steadily through the test, noting the time remaining from time to time. Don't panic if you are a little behind on your time schedule. Just work a little faster. Clear the cobwebs from your mind and write.

If you finish early, go back through and add or, if sure, change any answers or statements which seem wrong or weak when you read them. Remember, the teacher must evaluate what you put on paper, not what you "meant."

If time permits, check through again. This time be especially alert to correct any technical or grammatical weaknesses—incomplete sentences, punctuation, spelling, unclear writing, numbers, etc. Also make certain that you have numbered answers correctly, and that test pages are numbered and in the correct order.

Don't turn your paper in until the teacher requests it. That answer you're searching for in memory just could turn up suddenly, and it won't help your test score if your test is already turned in.

Basically, you should never be concerned with the whole test at any one moment. Conquer it question by question. If you should hit a mental block at some point, RELAX. Take a couple of deep breaths and read the next question doubly carefully. Above all, don't worry. Do your best.

TRUE-FALSE TESTS

The major secret for success with the true-false type test is extreme care in reading. Since most statements we read in textbooks and hear in lectures are "true," the true-false exam puts us in the rather novel situation of identifying and sifting out the false—the untrue. Your eyes can play tricks on you because of this "true" conditioning you experience in classes in general. They can momentarily be "blind" to a "no, not, never" in a statement, or think a cleverly stated near-truth is true.

Remember, if any question is not *totally* true, it must be considered false. There are no exceptions. There can be no half-truths in this type test.

In true-false tests, there is normally a large number of questions. Read each question very carefully, answer it to the best of your ability, then promptly move on to the next one. Most students find that it pays to let their intuitions help them on true-false tests, even if they do not consciously know which is the correct response.

If you have time to go back through the test, invariably doubts about some of your answers will creep in. These doubts can cause you to change answers which often will lower your score.

Therefore, *never* change any answer unless you are absolutely sure that your first response is incorrect for one of these reasons: (1) you carelessly misread the question the first time; (2) a later question gives a definite clue to indicate an error in an earlier response; (3) you answered in the wrong blank, or were guilty of another mechanical error. Don't change an answer for any other reasons.

Attempt all questions. Since you are graded by the number of correct responses, try those you don't know. You have a chance of getting some of those correct by guessing.

MULTIPLE-CHOICE TESTS

It has been said that multiple-choice tests are a manifestation of a sadistic mind. These exams can, indeed, be tricky. Again, careful reading is an absolute necessity. You must give your total attention to each question as you answer it. Read each question twice. Then read the question and each answer choice together. Carefully make your choice, and move to the next one. Be careful about making any changes if you have time to re-check your work.

ESSAY-TYPE TESTS

These are the bugaboo of many students. Essay tests call for more originality and creativity and organizational ability than do objective examinations.

Preview the test carefully and determine time allowances for each portion or question.

Concern yourself with only one question at a time. Start answering only after you are certain what is asked for. Are you to define? compare? contrast? explain? discuss? outline? list? give details? or what? Each of these terms or words demands a different type of response. Be sure you know what is expected and then go ahead.

If time permits, check back through your answers and make additions, changes, and routine corrections if necessary.

Since essay-type tests normally require more time than objective tests, it is most important that you begin as soon as the test is given to you, and work steadily and as rapidly as possible until you finish.

It Makes Sense

For all tests, prepare adequately in advance, don't worry, relax, begin work promptly, budget your time, read each question carefully, be concerned with only one question at a time, re-check your work if time permits, and don't turn in your paper until the teacher asks for it.

Appendix 3

Why This Method Works

The Cutler Accele*read* Method and techniques described and explained in *Triple Your Reading Speed* are based on the following premises:

I. The average reader can increase, by a minimum of three times, his reading rate of words per minute.

II. Reading is a skill, a developed or acquired ability.
  A. An acquired or developed ability can be developed further, refined, and improved.
  B. There must be a desire to improve that ability.
  C. A carefully worked out and proved course or program is essential to that improvement.
  D. Reading methods and patterns can and do become habit.
    1. In time, it is normal for the individual, without supervision, to acquire and fix, by continuous repetition, slow reading habits and practices.
    2. More often than not, primary instruction in basic oral and forced silent reading tends to fix the normal or regular silent reading rate at or near the oral reading (speech) rate of approximately 150 words per minute.
    3. Vocalization and sub-vocalization—reading more or less aloud, or reading aloud "silently" is the practice which is usually learned by the beginning reader.
    4. Once the oral reader learns to real silently, there is rarely any further instruction in reading throughout the entire educational experience.

III. Reading rate may be increased by either or both of two means:
  A. If the individual, over an extended period, reads voluminously.
  B. If the individual has specialized instruction to increase his rate.

IV. Reading rate is determined primarily by the deviations of eye fixations made per line of print by the individual reader.
  A. It is necessary to minimize the number of eye stops in order to achieve marked increases in rate.
    1. Conscious and deliberate control of the eyes must be gained.
    2. The vision consciousness (eye-span) area must be increased.
    3. A regular, systematic method for visually covering printed matter must be developed.
    4. Drill and practice with faster, more efficient methods is necessary.

V. Reading rate (and comprehension) is further determined by other reasons and conditions.
   A. The reader's basic intelligence, coordination, and visual acquity.
   B. The type of material being read.
   C. The purpose(s) for which the material is read.
   D. The reader's familiarity with the field or subject.
   E. The degree of the reader's interest.
   F. The reader's attitude toward reading in general, and the subject in particular.
   G. The reader's immediate state of health, fatigue, comfort, etc.
   H. The reader's previous reading experience, or lack of it.
VI. Reading is primarily a mental activity. (To a lesser degree, it is also a physical one.)
   A. An activity—mental or physical—requires the expenditure of energy.
   B. Prolonged, or sustained exertion of energy will produce fatigue.
   C. Fatigue, either mental or physical, normally lessens the ability to concentrate.
   D. Reducing the time required to read a given amount of material will aid comprehension by actually reducing fatigue, both mental and physical.
VII. The overall meaning and importance of a story, play, book, letter, etc., cannot be fully understood until the entire content has been read.
   A. Reading at a faster rate will enable the individual to see the "whole" more quickly, thereby improving understanding.
   B. The individual's thinking rate far exceeds his speech rate of approximately 150 words per minute.
VIII. Few students know how to study effectively; teaching the student proper study habits will result in more productive study time, and better comprehension for that individual.

Test Answers

Inventory Test 1—(Value: 4 points each) 1,230 Words
(1) e (2) d (3) c (4) b (5) e (6) c (7) c (8) a (9) e (10) b (11) b (12) d (13) e (14) e (15) d (16) d (17) a (18) b (19) d (20) e (21) d (22) c (23) e (24) b (25) d

Inventory Test 2—(Value: 4 points each) 1,140 Words
(1) e (2) d (3) c (4) b (5) e (6) c (7) c (8) a (9) e (10) b (11) b (12) d (13) e (14) e (15) d (16) d (17) a (18) b (19) d (20) e (21) d (22) c (23) e (24) b (25) d

Test—*The Web of Life*—(Value: 10 points each) Approximately 2,400 Words
(1) d (2) c (3) a (4) d (5) b (6) b (7) d (8) b (9) a (10) a

Test— The Cask of Amontillado—(Value: 10 points each) Approximately 2,600 Words
(1) b (2) a (3) c (4) c (5) b (6) b (7) b (8) a (9) c (10) d

Test—*A Short History of the Civil War*—(Value: 4 points each) Approximately 4,300 Words
(1) a (2) b (3) d (4) b (5) c (6) a (7) d (8) c (9) a (10) b (11) d (12) a (13) b (14) b (15) a (16) b (17) c (18) d (19) b (20) a (21) a (22) c (23) b (24) c (25) a

Test—*Treasure Island*—(Value: 5 points each) Approximately 2,400 Words
(1) T (2) F (3) F (4) T (5) F (6) F (7) T (8) F (9) F (10) F (11) F (12) T (13) F (14) T (15) F (16) T (17) T (18) F (19) F (20) T

Test—*Time Machine*—(Value: 3 points each) Approximately 6,600 Words
(1) T (2) F (3) T (4) F (5) T (6) T (7) F (8) T (9) F (10) F (11) F (12) T
(13) F (14) T (15) F (16) T (17) F (18) T (19) T (20) F (21) T (22) T
(23) F (24) T (25) T (26) F (27) F (28) F (29) T (30) T (31) T (32) T
(33) T

Test—*Dr. Jekyll and Mr. Hyde*—(Value: 4 points each) Approximately 7,000 Words
(1) d (2) b (3) a (4) d (5) b (6) c (7) a (8) d (9) a (10) d (11) b (12) b
(13) a (14) d (15) b (16) d (17) b (18) a (19) a (20) d (21) b (22) d (23) c
(24) a (25) b